RECORDED VERSIONS
GUITAR

AUTHENTIC TRANSCRIPTIONS
WITH NOTES AND TABLATURE

AUDIOSLAVE - REVELATIONS

Music transcriptions by Pete Billmann

ISBN-13: 978-1-4234-2446-8
ISBN-10: 1-4234-2446-8

HAL•LEONARD®
CORPORATION

7777 W. BLUEMOUND RD. P.O. BOX 13819 MILWAUKEE, WI 53213

In Australia Contact:
Hal Leonard Australia Pty. Ltd.
4 Lentara Court
Cheltenham, Victoria, 3192 Australia
Email: ausadmin@halleonard.com

4   REVELATIONS

13   ONE AND THE SAME

19   SOUND OF A GUN

25   UNTIL WE FALL

32   ORIGINAL FIRE

38   BROKEN CITY

47   SOMEDAYS

55   SHAPE OF THINGS TO COME

64   JEWEL OF THE SUMMERTIME

70   WIDE AWAKE

78   NOTHING LEFT TO SAY BUT GOODBYE

83   MOTH

90   GUITAR NOTATION LEGEND

Revelations

Lyrics by Chris Cornell
Music written and arranged by Audioslave

Tune down 1 step:
(low to high) D-G-C-F-A-D

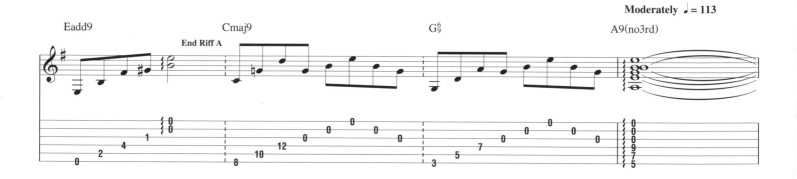

*Doubled throughout
***Vol. swell

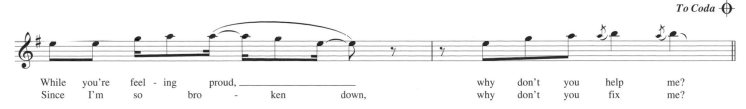

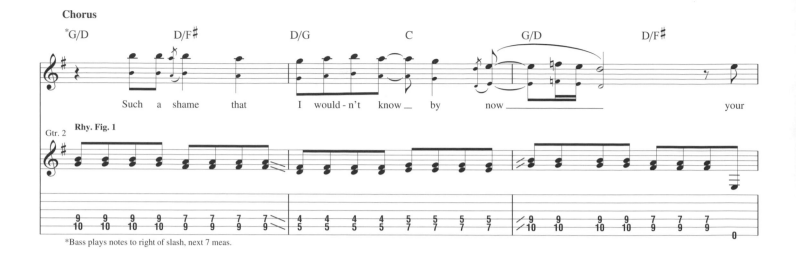

*Bass plays notes to right of slash, next 7 meas.

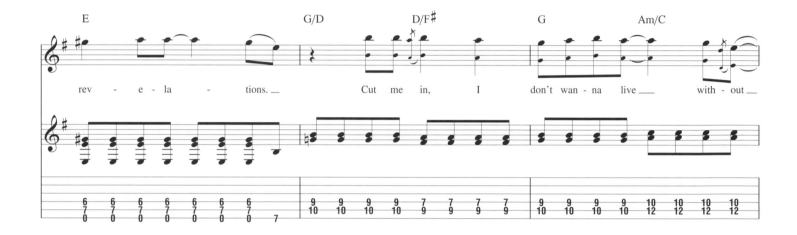

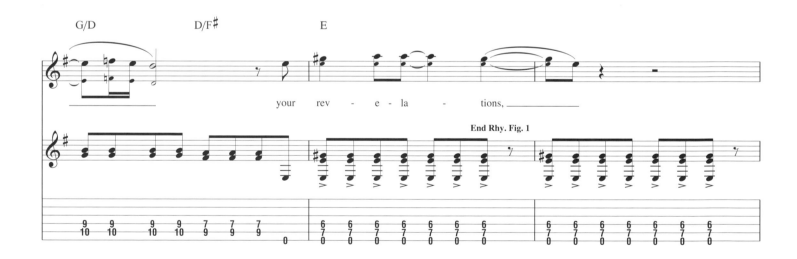

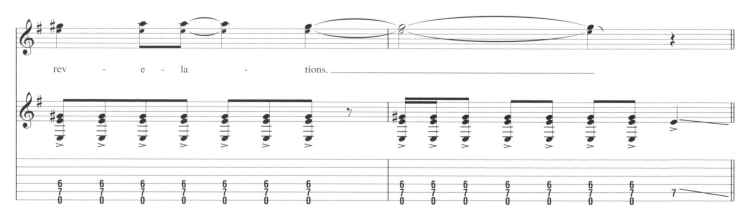

Interlude
Gtr. 2: w/ Riff B (2 times)

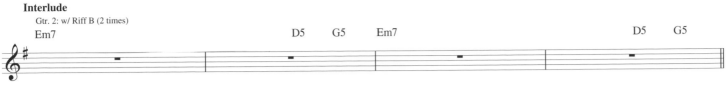

⊕ **Coda**
Chorus
Gtr. 2: w/ Rhy. Fig. 1

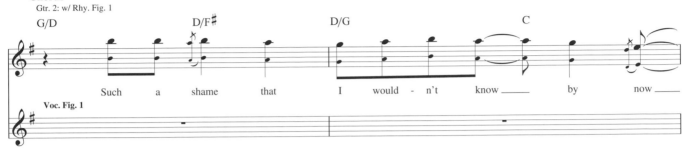

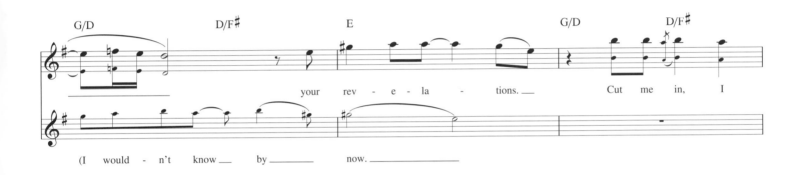

Guitar Solo

*Using a guitar with Les Paul style electronics, set lead volume to 0 and rhythm volume to 10. Hammer-on the strings with the left hand while flipping
the pickup selector switch in a sixteenth-note rhythm until beat 4 of the 7th meas. Delay set for a time value equal to 5 sixteenth-notes w/ 1 repeat.
Delayed signal sent to right channel. Whammy pedal set for one octave above. Press the Whammy's on/off switch in the rhythm indicated
(+ = on, o = off). Whammy effect in left channel only.

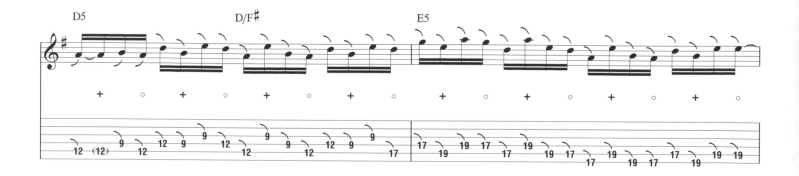

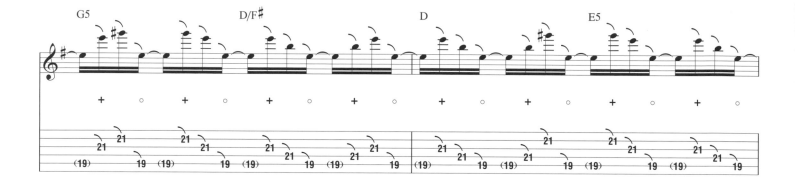

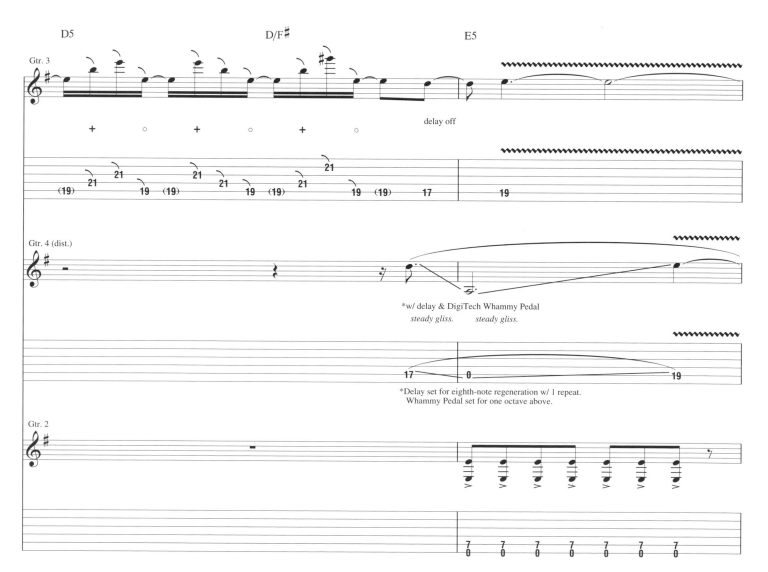

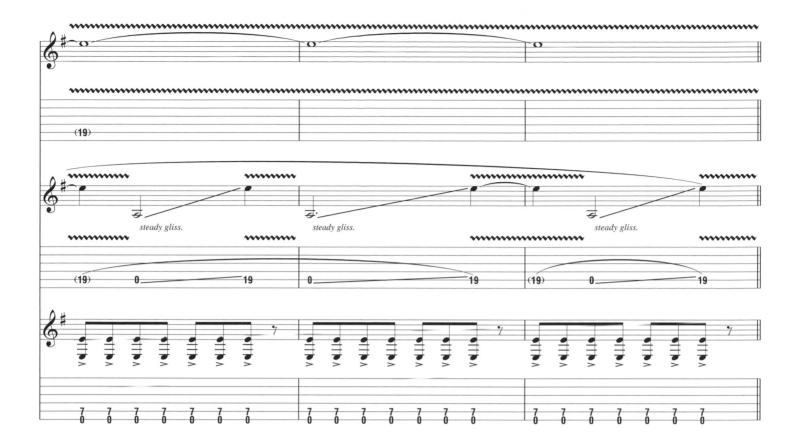

Bridge

Half-time feel

Gtr. 1: w/ Riff A (3 times)
Gtrs. 2, 3 & 4 tacet

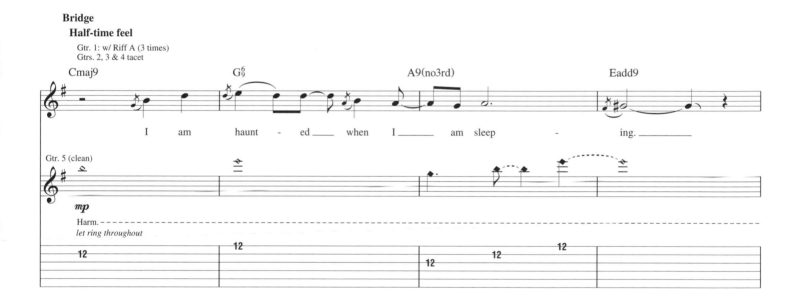

Cmaj9   G⁶/₉   A9(no3rd)   Eadd9

I   am   haunt - ed ___ when I ___ am sleep - ing. ___

Gtr. 5 (clean)

mp

Harm. -
let ring throughout

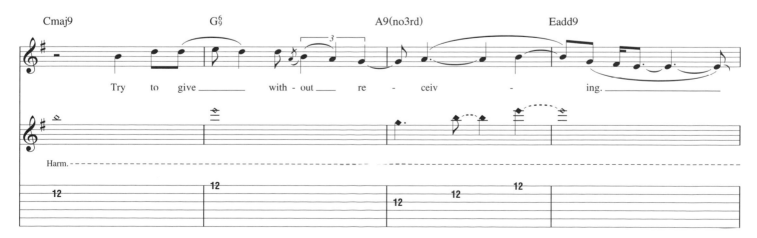

Cmaj9   G⁶/₉   A9(no3rd)   Eadd9

Try   to   give ___ with - out ___ re - ceiv - ing. ___

Harm. -

It's in the ap - ple bite, _____ it's in the days and nights. _____

(It's in the ap - ple bite, _____ it's in _____ the

Harm. -

Pitch: E

In the af - ter - life _____ we'll _____ meet.

days and nights.) _____

Gtr. 5

Harm. -

Gtr. 1

Interlude

Gtrs. 1 & 5 tacet

Gtr. 2

Rhy. Fig. 2

End Rhy. Fig. 2

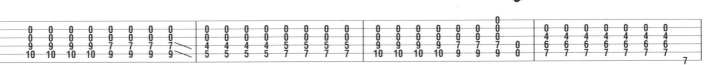

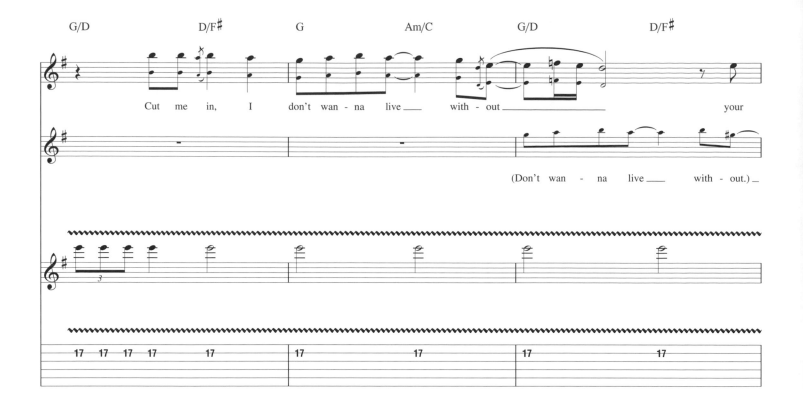

Cut me in, I don't wan - na live ___ with - out _____ your

(Don't wan - na live ___ with - out.) __

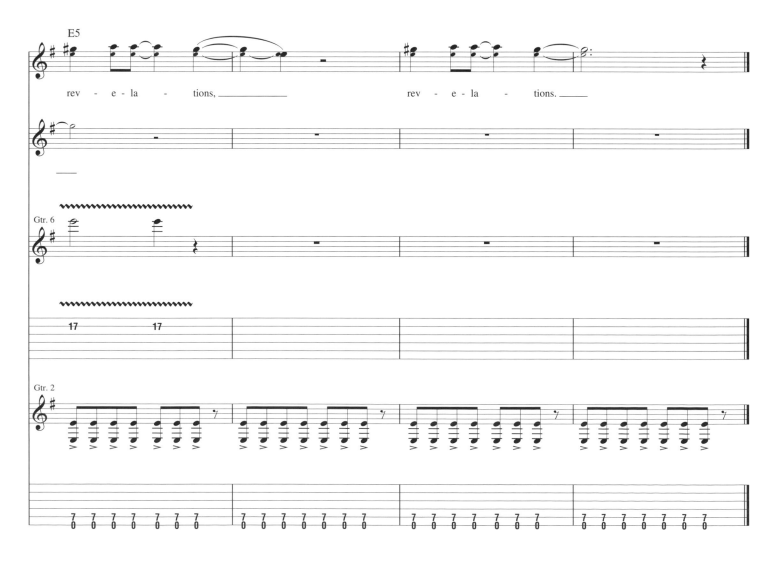

rev - e - la - tions, _____ rev - e - la - tions. _____

Gtr. 6

Gtr. 2

One and the Same

Lyrics by Chris Cornell
Music written and arranged by Audioslave

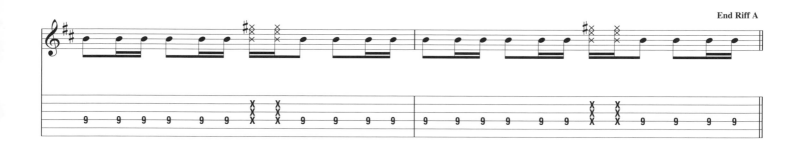

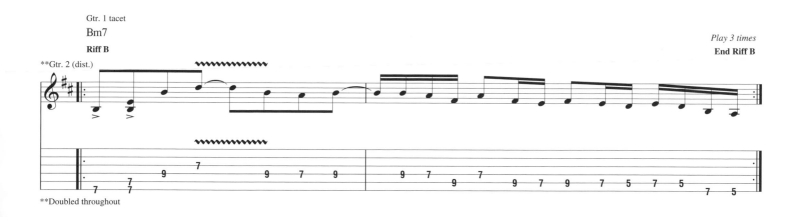

1. Well, they don't

§ **Verse**

hate you, _____ you know they love you, _____ but they're
mask _____ with a tar - get. _____ Keep your

*Key signature denotes B Mixolydian.

Rhy. Fig. 1

Gtr. 2

gon - na come kill you. _____ They _____ don't _____
en - e - mies clos - er. _____ You fall in

End Rhy. Fig. 1

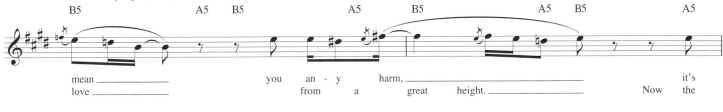

Gtr. 2: w/ Rhy. Fig. 1 (2 times)

mean _____ you an - y harm, _____ it's
love _____ from a great height. _____ Now the

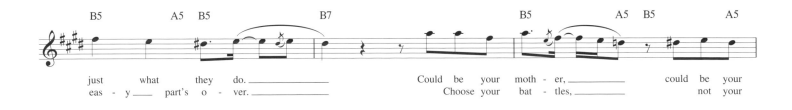

just what they do. _____ Could be your moth - er, _____ could be your
eas - y _____ part's o - ver. _____ Choose your bat - tles, _____ not your

To Coda 1

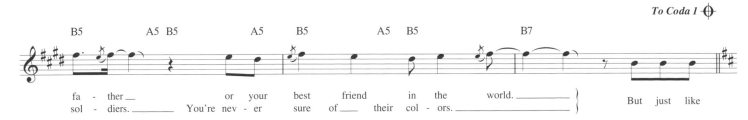

fa - ther _____ or your best friend in the world. _____ } But just like
sol - diers. _____ You're nev - er sure of _____ their col - ors. _____ }

Guitar Solo

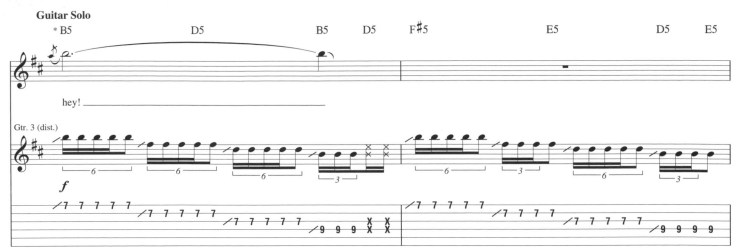

hey! _____

*Chord symbols implied by bass, next 8 meas.

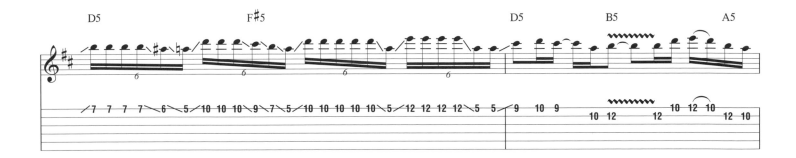

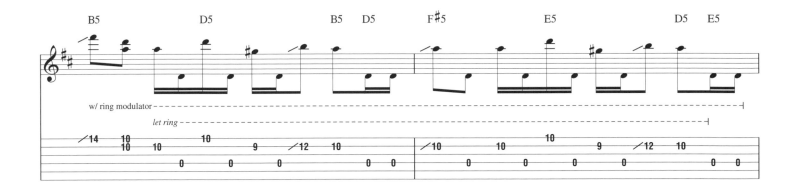

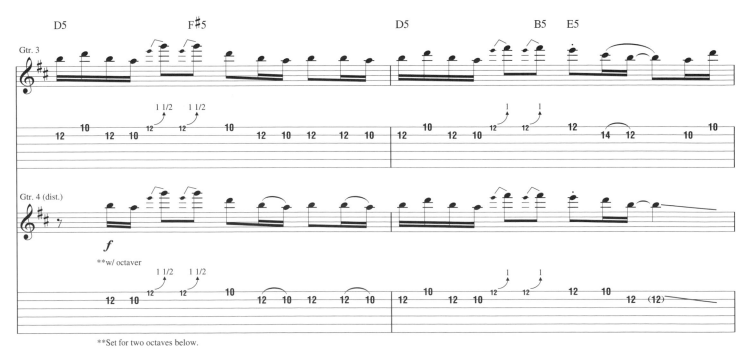

**Set for two octaves below.

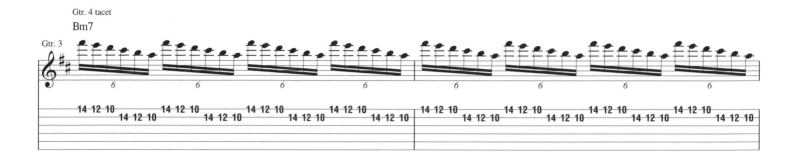

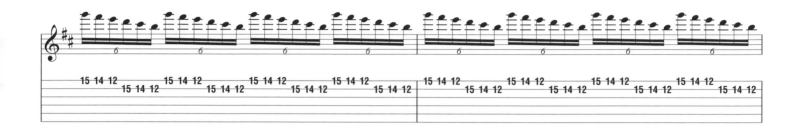

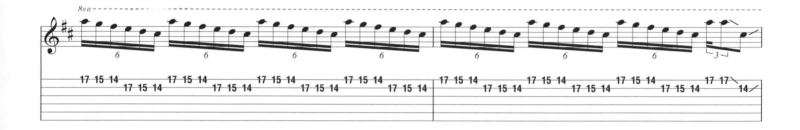

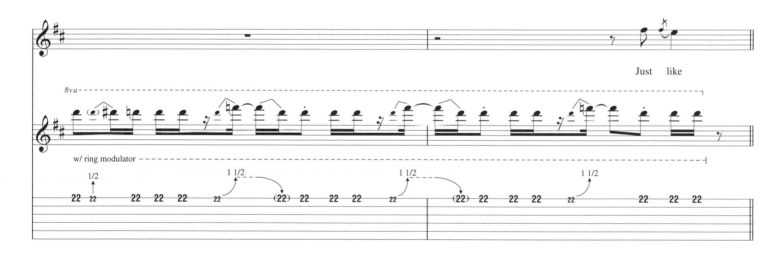

Just like

Chorus

Gtr. 3 tacet

blood in _____ rain, _____ love and pain _____ are

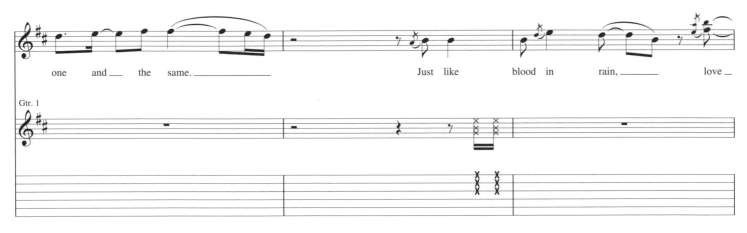

one and the same. Just like blood in rain, love

Gtr. 1

D.S.S. al Coda 2

and pain are one in the same. Just like a

(One in the same.)

1.

⊕ Coda 2

Outro

Gtr. 2: w/ Riff B (3 times)

Bm7

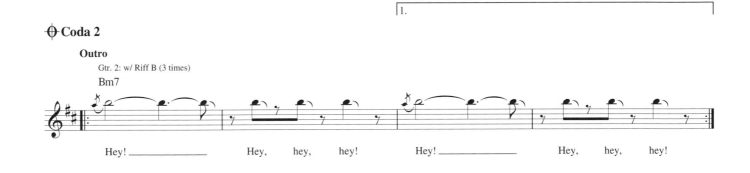

Hey! Hey, hey, hey! Hey! Hey, hey, hey!

2.

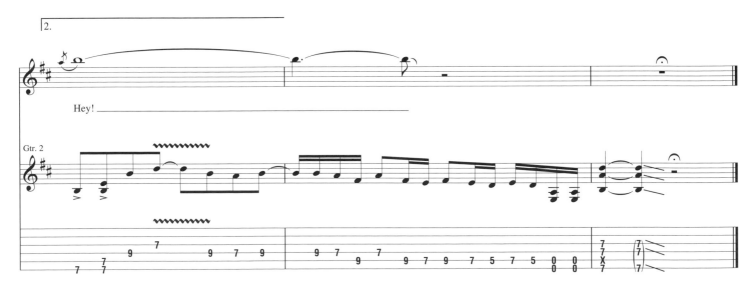

Hey!

Gtr. 2

Sound of a Gun

Lyrics by Chris Cornell
Music written and arranged by Audioslave

Drop D tuning:
(low to high) D-A-D-G-B-E

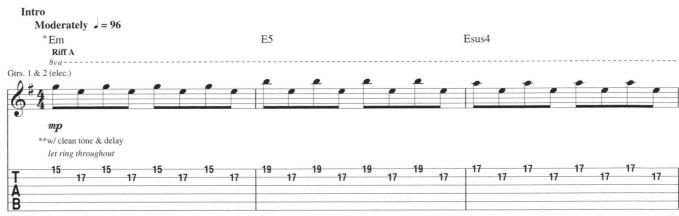

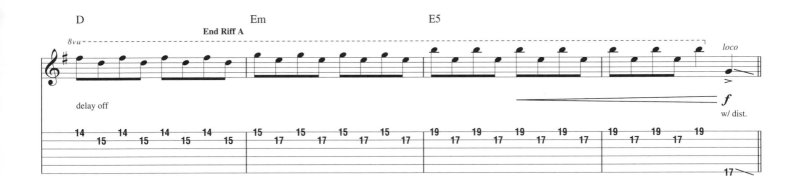

*Chord symbols reflect implied harmony.

**Delay set for dotted eighth-note regeneration w/ 1 repeat.

Verse

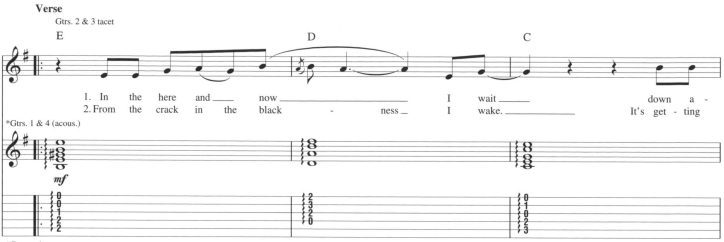

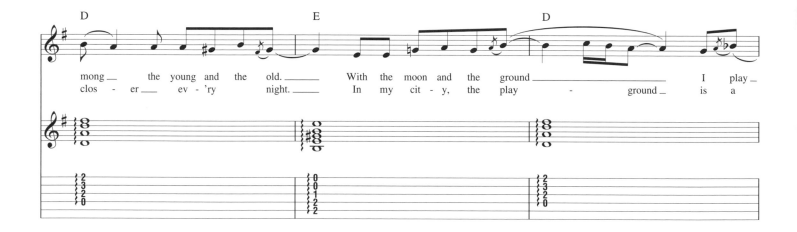

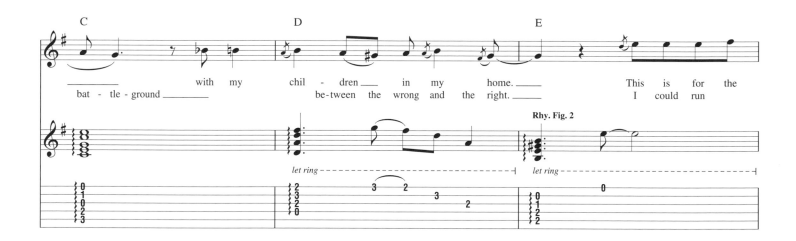

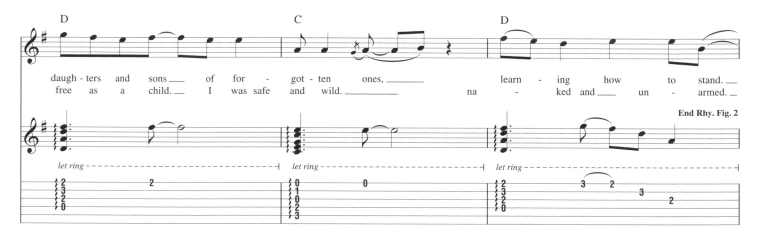

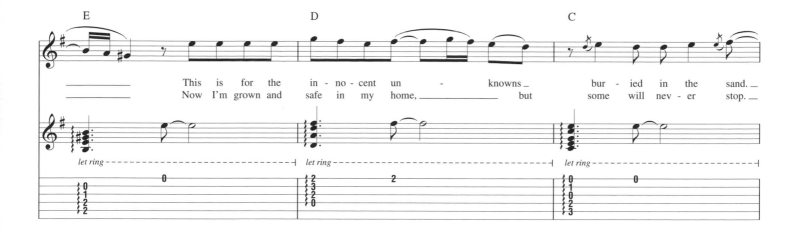

Chorus

Gtr. 4 tacet

1st time, Gtr. 3: w/ Rhy. Fig. 1A (2 times)
2nd time, Gtr. 3: w/ Rhy. Fig. 1A (1 1/2 times)

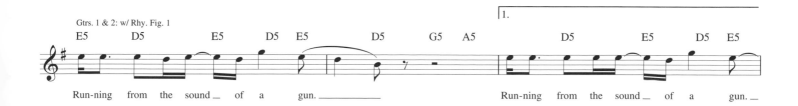

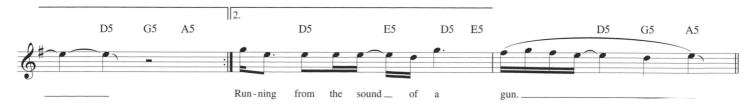

Guitar Solo

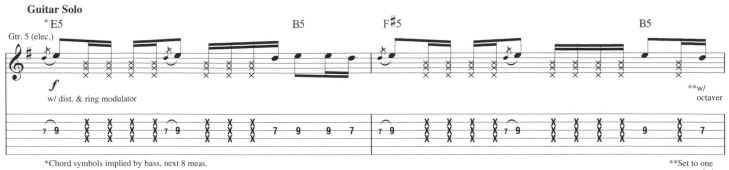

*Chord symbols implied by bass, next 8 meas.

**Set to one octave below.

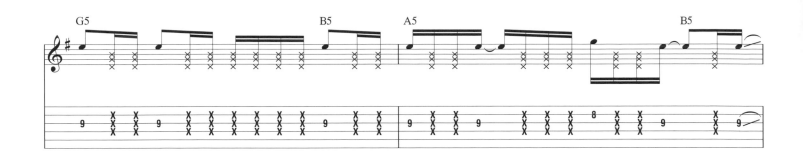

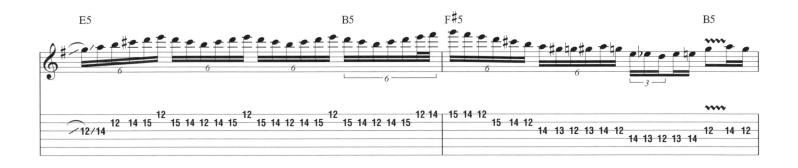

Bridge

***Gtrs. 1 & 2: w/ Riff A

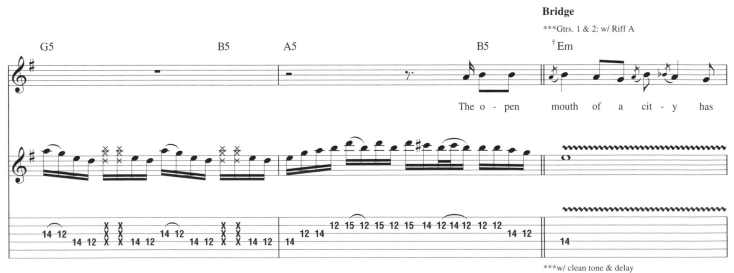

The o - pen mouth of a cit - y has

***w/ clean tone & delay

†Chord symbols reflect overall harmony.

swal-lowed up a town. _ Well, that same old _ con - crete that I still _ walk down. _ And it

seemed they put a shine ___ on this place when I ___ was young, ___ or

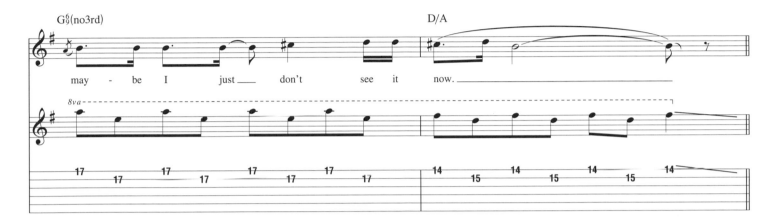

may - be I just ___ don't see it now.

Chorus

*Gtrs. 1 & 4: w/ Rhy. Fig. 2 (1 1/2 times)
Gtr. 2 tacet

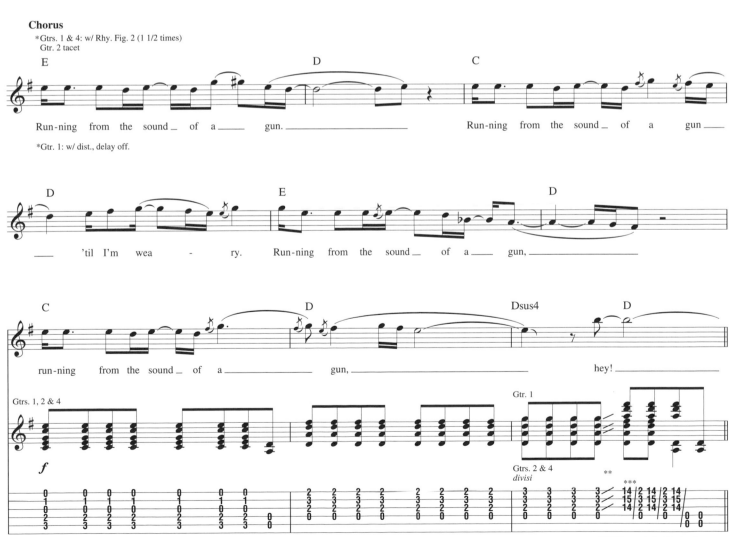

Run-ning from the sound ___ of a ___ gun. ___ Run-ning from the sound ___ of a gun ___

*Gtr. 1: w/ dist., delay off.

___ 'til I'm wea - ry. Run-ning from the sound ___ of a ___ gun, ___

run-ning from the sound ___ of a ___ gun, ___ hey!

Gtrs. 1, 2 & 4

Gtr. 1

Gtrs. 2 & 4
divisi

**Slides apply to Gtr. 1 only.
*** Gtr. 1 to left of slashes in tab.

Interlude

*w/ wah-wah in the toe down position.

Outro-Chorus

Run - ning   from   the   sound ___   of   a ___   gun, ___

run - ning   from   the   sound ___   of   a ___   gun. ___

Run - ning   from   the   sound ___   of   a   gun, ___   a

run-ning from, ___   run-ning from ___   the   sound   of ___   a ___   gun. ___

24

Until We Fall

Lyrics by Chris Cornell
Music written and arranged by Audioslave

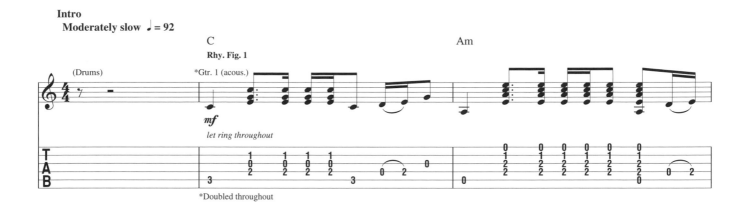

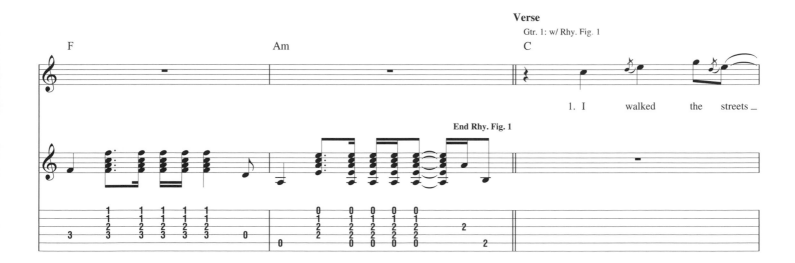

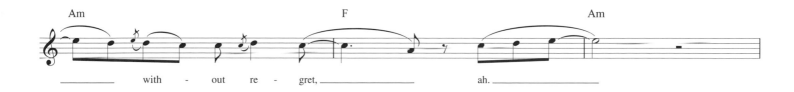

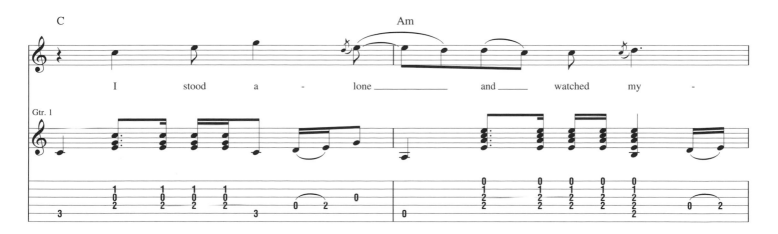

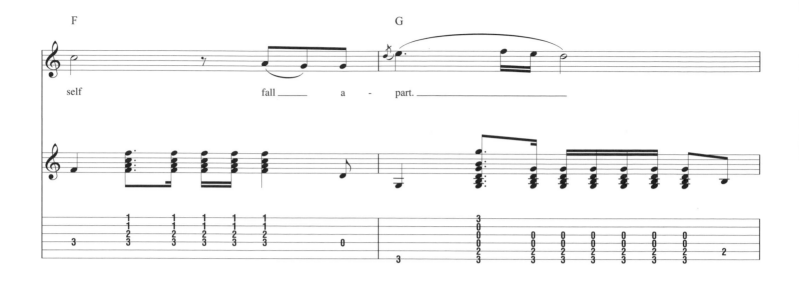

self   fall   a - part.

Gtr. 1: w/ Rhy. Fig. 1 (1 1/2 times)

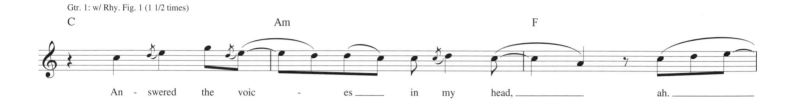

An - swered   the   voic   -   es   in   my   head,   ah.

Slipped   through   the   chain   -   link   of   a   bro -

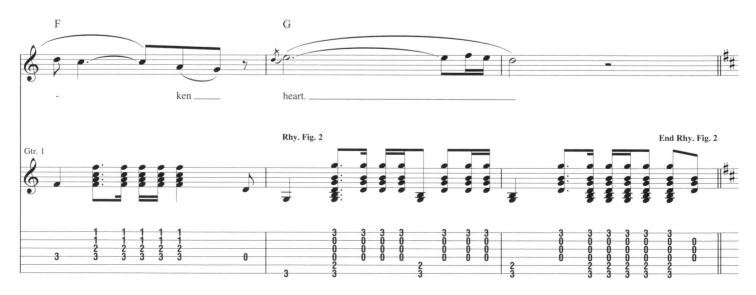

- ken   heart.

Rhy. Fig. 2   End Rhy. Fig. 2

Gtr. 1

Chorus

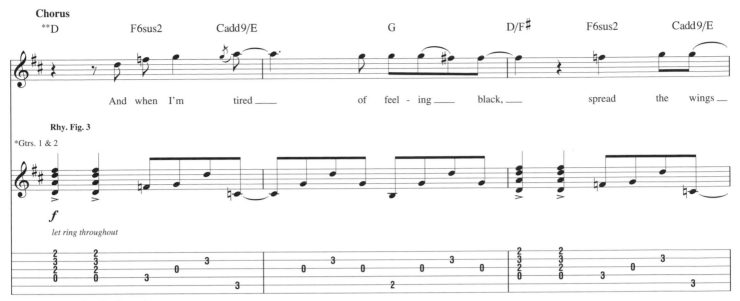

And when I'm tired ____ of feel-ing ____ black, ____ spread the wings ____

*Gtr. 2 (elec.) w/ slight dist. Composite arrangement

**Chord symbols reflect overall harmony.

____ up - on ____ your back. ____ Take us high ____ a - bove it all, ____

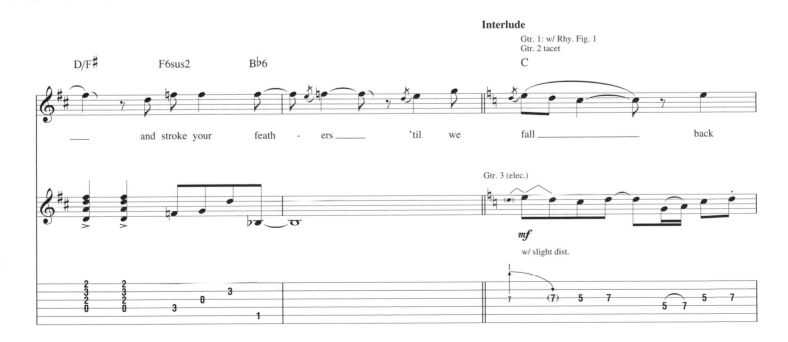

____ and stroke your feath - ers ____ 'til we fall ____ back

down ___ a - gain, _____ ah. _____

Verse

Gtrs. 1 & 2: w/ Rhy. Fig. 1 (1 3/4 times)

Gtr. 3 tacet

2. Bought ev - 'ry - thing _____ that ___ sound - ed good, ___ ah. _____

___ I un - der - stand _____ that ___ I've been ___ mis -

Gtrs. 1 & 2: w/ Rhy. Fig. 2

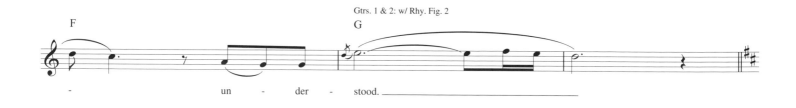

- un - der - stood. _____

𝄋 Chorus

Gtrs. 1 & 2: w/ Rhy. Fig. 3 (1 1/2 times)

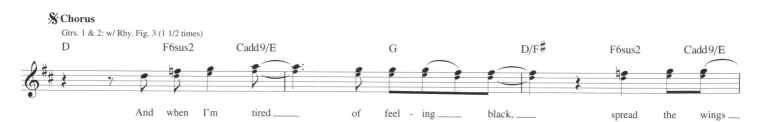

And when I'm tired ___ of feel - ing ___ black, ___ spread the wings ___

28

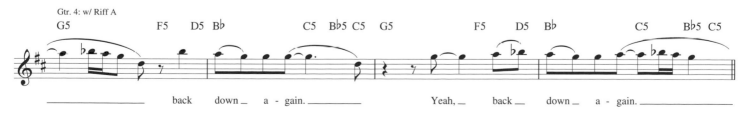

Bridge

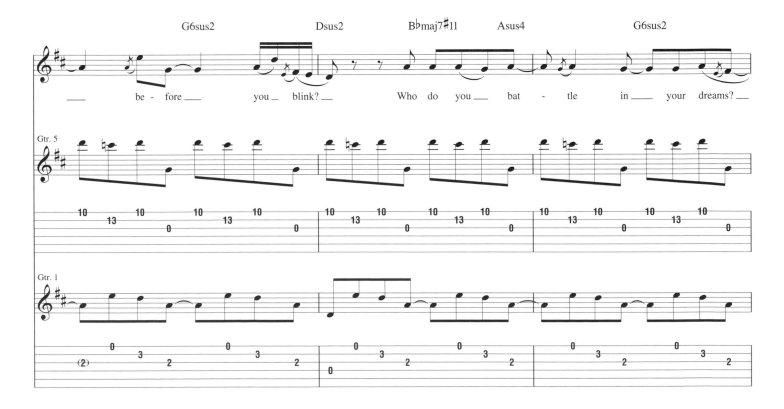

Original Fire

Lyrics by Chris Cornell
Music written and arranged by Audioslave

1.
Gtr. 1: w/ Rhy. Fig. 2

rig - i - nal fire ___ has died _____ and gone, ___ but the ri - ot in - side ___ moves on. ___

Interlude
Gtr. 1   E5

2.
Gtr. 1: w/ Rhy. Fig. 2

rig - i - nal fire ___ has died ___ and long gone, ___ but the ri - ot in - side ___ moves ___ on. ___

Bridge

A5   E5   G5   A5   B5   D5

Can't ex - plain ___ it, it was some - thin' to see. ___ Can't con - tain ___ some - thin' ev - er ___

Gtr. 1   **Riff C**   **End Riff C**

E5   B5   D5

re -   al,   ev - er

*Gtr. 1: w/ Riff A

E7(no3rd)   E6(no3rd)   C/E   E5

re -   al.   Hey! ___

*w/ Whammy pedal as before.

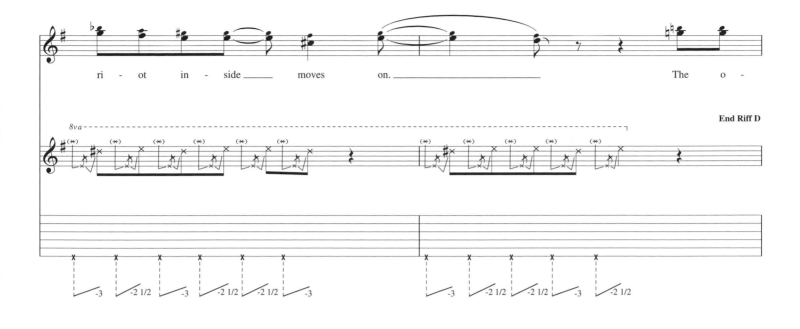

ri - ot in - side ____ moves on. _____ The o -

End Riff D

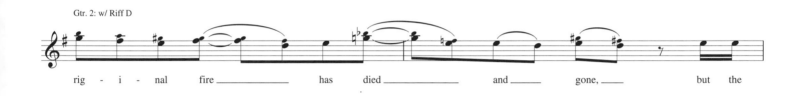

Gtr. 2: w/ Riff D

rig - i - nal fire _____ has died _____ and _____ gone, _____ but the

ri - ot in - side ____ moves ____ on. _____

Gtr. 1

Broken City

Lyrics by Chris Cornell
Music written and arranged by Audioslave

build - ing falls, _____ you would-n't care to no - tice un - less you were in _____ it. And

no one _____ cares _____ a - bout climb - ing stairs, _____ noth - ing at the top no more.

Chorus

Gtr. 1 tacet

| D5 | | C5 | D5 | C5 | D5 | C5 | D5 | | C5 | D5 | C5 | D5 | C5 |

Out - side trip-pin' in the bro - ken cit - y. _____

Riff B1

End Riff B1

Gtr. 3 (dist.)

f

*w/ phaser & DigiTech Whammy Pedal

*Set for one octave above.

Riff B

End Riff B

Gtr. 2 (dist.)

f

w/ phaser

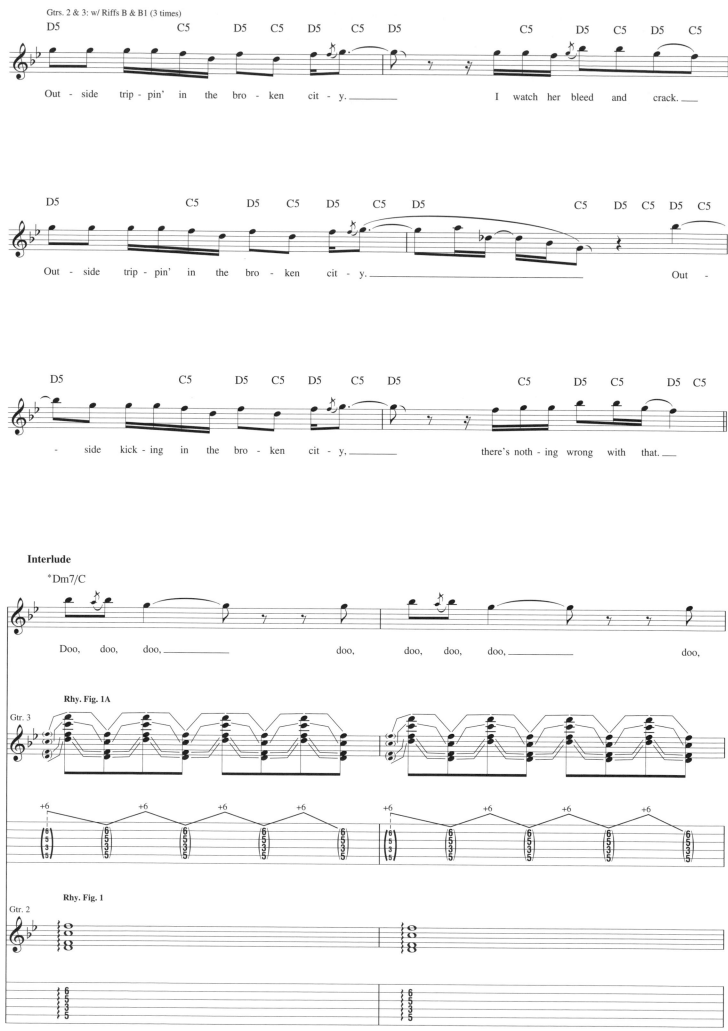

Gtrs. 2 & 3: w/ Riffs B & B1 (3 times)

Out - side trip - pin' in the bro - ken cit - y. _____ I watch her bleed and crack. ____

Out - side trip - pin' in the bro - ken cit - y. _____ Out -

- side kick - ing in the bro - ken cit - y, _____ there's noth - ing wrong with that. ___

Interlude

Doo, doo, doo, _____ doo, doo, doo, doo, _____ doo,

Rhy. Fig. 1A

Gtr. 3

Rhy. Fig. 1

Gtr. 2

*Bass plays C.

40

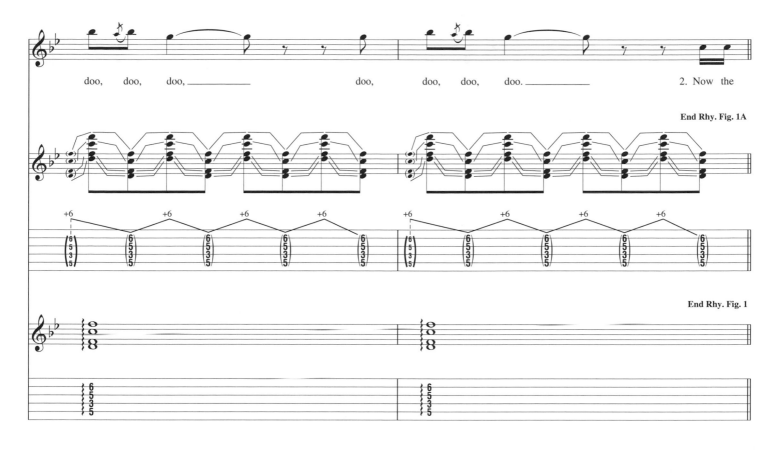

doo, doo, doo, _____ doo, doo, doo, doo. _____ 2. Now the

End Rhy. Fig. 1A

End Rhy. Fig. 1

Verse

Gtr. 1: w/ Riff A (2 times)
Gtrs. 2 & 3 tacet

G5

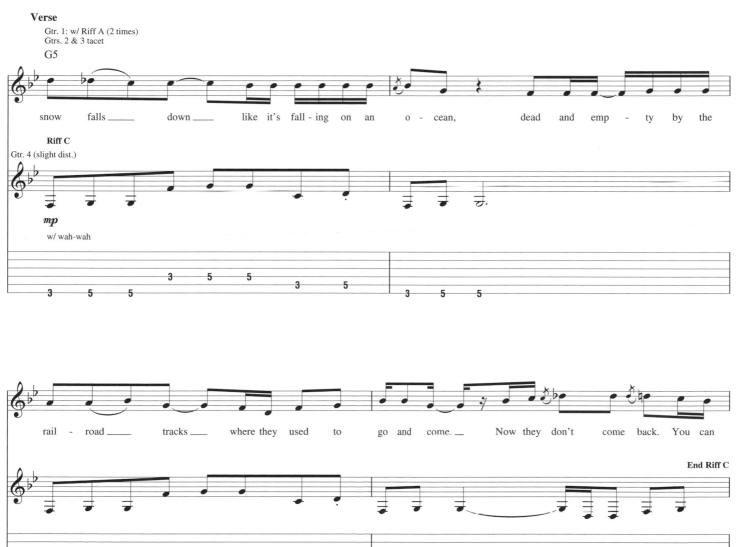

snow falls _____ down _____ like it's fall-ing on an o-cean, dead and emp-ty by the

Riff C
Gtr. 4 (slight dist.)

mp

w/ wah-wah

rail-road _____ tracks _____ where they used to go and come. ___ Now they don't come back. You can

End Riff C

Gtr. 4: w/ Riff C

hear the rust _____ grow-ing up the through-ways, down the al - leys where they

stole this town _____ from the fron-tier. I can see him try'n' to steal it back.

Chorus

Gtrs. 2 & 3: w/ Riffs B & B1 (4 times)

D5   C5   D5   C5   D5   C5   D5   C5   D5   C5   D5   C5

Out - side trip - pin' in the bro - ken cit - y. _____

Voc. Fig. 1

(Out - side trip - pin' in the bro - ken cit - y.) _____

D5   C5   D5   C5   D5   C5   D5   C5   D5   C5   D5   C5

Out - side trip - pin' in the bro - ken cit - y. _____ I watch her bleed and crack. _____

End Voc. Fig. 1

Bkgd. Voc.: w/ Voc. Fig. 1

D5   C5   D5   C5   D5   C5   D5   C5   D5   C5   D5   C5

Out - side kick - ing in the bro - ken cit - y. _____ Out -

Interlude

Gtrs. 2 & 3: w/ Rhy. Figs. 1 & 1A

D5   C5   D5 C5 D5 C5 D5   C5   D5 C5   D5 C5   Dm7/C

- side trip-pin' in the bro - ken cit - y, there's noth-ing wrong with that. _____ Doo, doo, doo, _____ doo,

doo, doo, doo, _____ doo, doo, doo, doo, _____ doo, doo, doo, doo. _____ Doo,

42

Verse

Gtr. 1: w/ Riff D (4 times)
Gtr. 6: w/ Rhy. Fig. 2 (4 times)

Gtr. 5 tacet

sun won't shine ___ on this part of the map ___ an - y - more. ___ When it's

steady gliss.

cold out - side ___ I see it hide be - hind the smoke - stacks, ___ noth - ing grows. ___ There's no

gold rush, no min - er, no rev - o - lu - tion be - hind her ___ and the

ship - yard is a grave - yard. No one will be try'n' to find ___ her. ___

Chorus

Bkgd. Voc.: w/ Voc. Fig. 1 (2 times)
Gtrs. 2 & 3: w/ Riffs B & B1 (4 times)

Out - side trip - pin' in the bro - ken cit - y. ___

Out - side kick - ing in the bro - ken cit - y. ___ I watch her bleed and crack. ___

Out - side trip - pin' in the bro - ken cit - y. ___ Out -

44

Gtr. 1: w/ Riff E (till fade)

Hey, _____ out - side trip - pin' in the bro - ken cit - y. _____

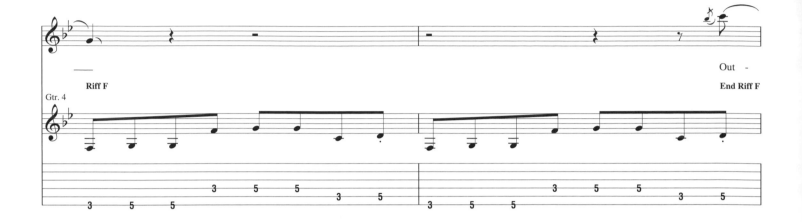

____ Out -

Riff F

Gtr. 4

End Riff F

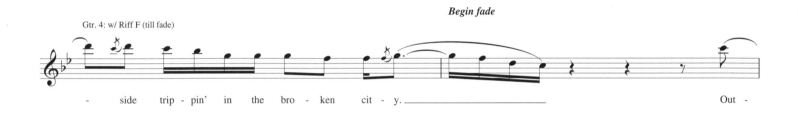

Gtr. 4: w/ Riff F (till fade)

Begin fade

- side trip - pin' in the bro - ken cit - y. _____ Out -

- side, _____ out - side, _____ out - side, _____ out - side. _____

Gtr. 5

Fade out

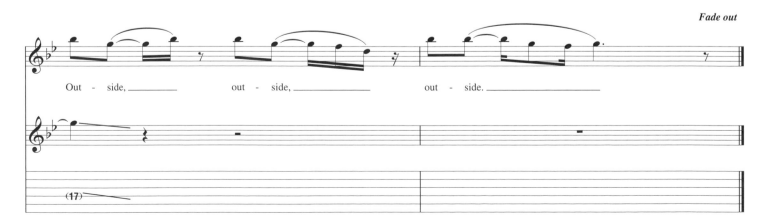

Out - side, _____ out - side, _____ out - side. _____

Somedays

Lyrics by Chris Cornell
Music written and arranged by Audioslave

Tune down 1/2 step:
(low to high) Eb-Ab-Db-Gb-Bb-Eb

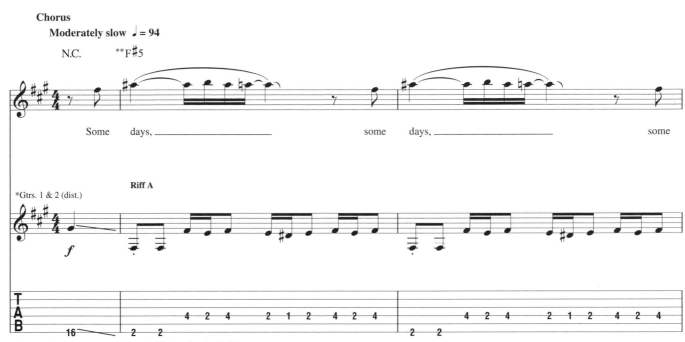

*Composite arrangement **Chord symbols reflect implied harmony.

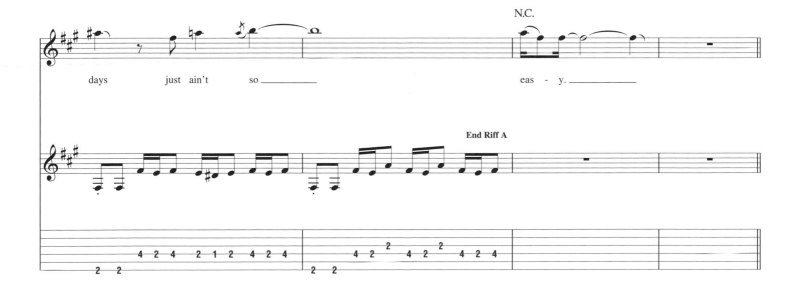

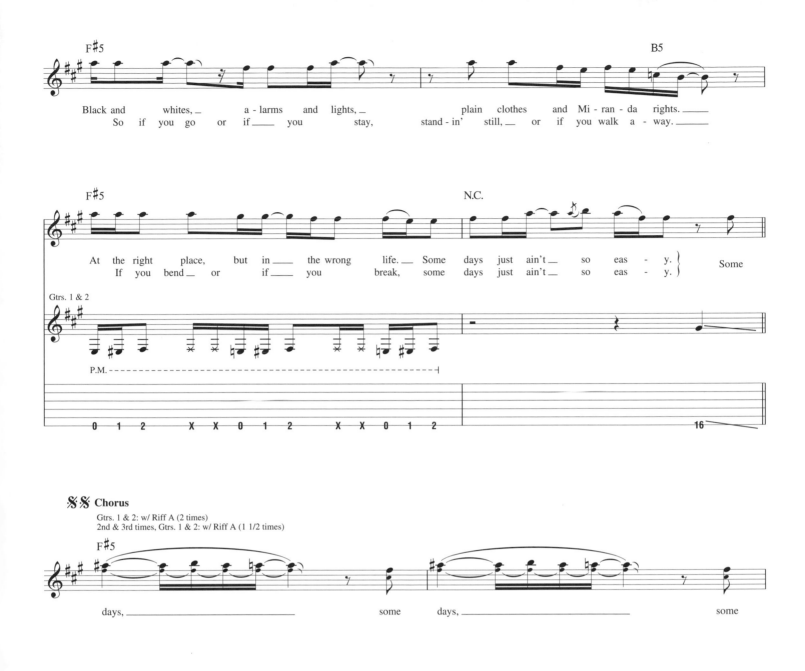

Black and whites, ___ a-larms and lights, ___ plain clothes and Mi - ran - da rights. ___
So if you go or if ___ you stay, stand - in' still, ___ or if you walk a - way. ___

At the right place, but in ___ the wrong life. ___ Some days just ain't ___ so eas - y.
If you bend ___ or if ___ you break, some days just ain't ___ so eas - y.

Some

Gtrs. 1 & 2

P.M. -------------------------------------

𝄋𝄋 Chorus

Gtrs. 1 & 2: w/ Riff A (2 times)
2nd & 3rd times, Gtrs. 1 & 2: w/ Riff A (1 1/2 times)

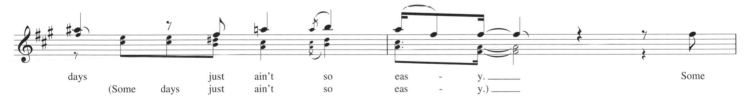

days, _____ some days, _____ some

days just ain't so eas - y. ___ Some
(Some days just ain't so eas - y.) ___

To Coda 1 ⊕
To Coda 2 ⊕

days, _____ some days, _____ some

days, some days just ain't so
(Some days, some days just ain't so

Interlude

⊕ Coda

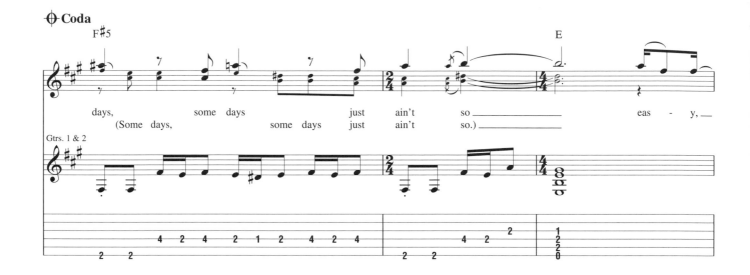

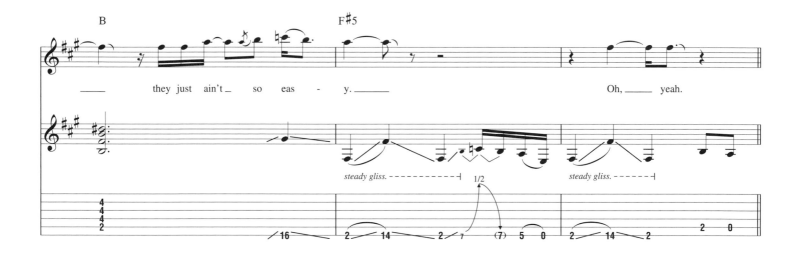

Bridge

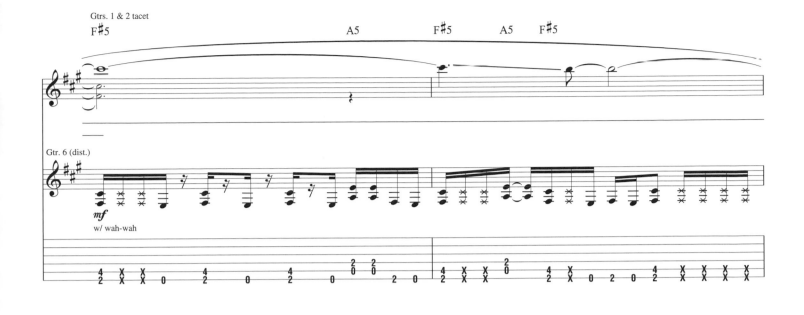

Guitar Solo

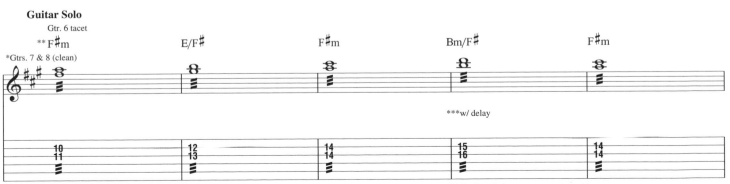

*Gtr. 8 w/ heavy reverb, played *mf*.

**Chord symbols reflect overall harmony.

***Set for whole-note regeneration w/ 1 repeat.

Bridge

Some - one may have done you right or done you wrong, _____

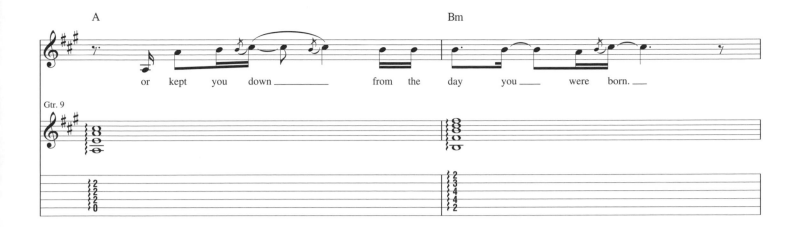

or kept you down _____ from the day you _____ were born. _____

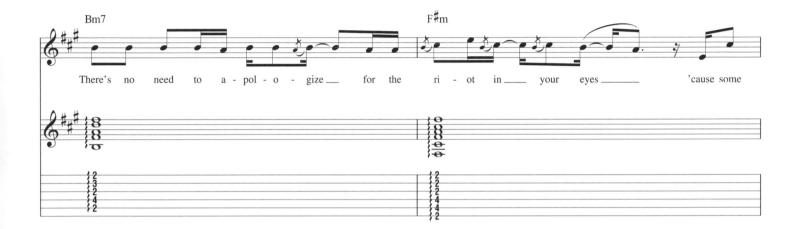

There's no need to a-pol-o-gize _____ for the ri-ot in _____ your eyes _____ 'cause some

days just ain't _____ so eas - y.

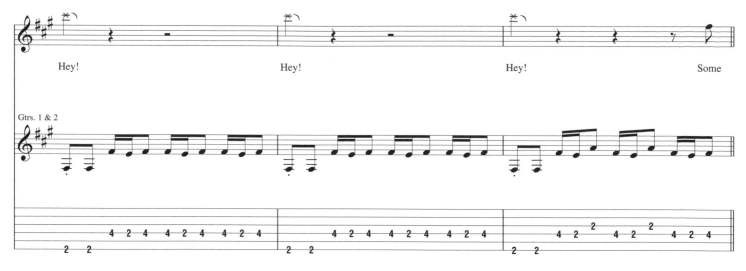

Hey!　　　　　Hey!　　　　　Hey!　　　　　Some

Coda 2

days,　　　some days　　　　just ain't　　so
(Some days,　　　some days.)

Pitch: C#

Free time

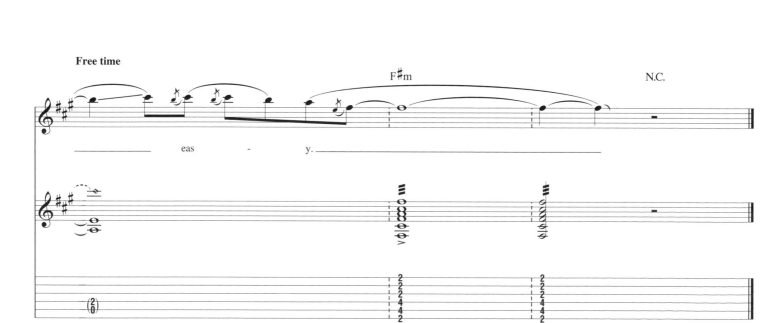

eas - y.

Shape of Things to Come

Lyrics by Chris Cornell
Music written and arranged by Audioslave

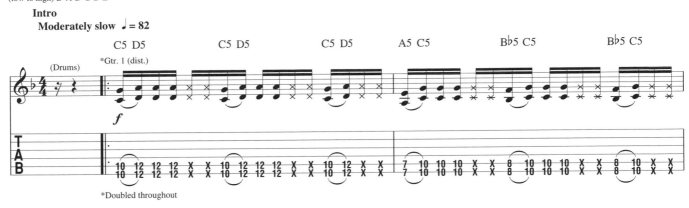

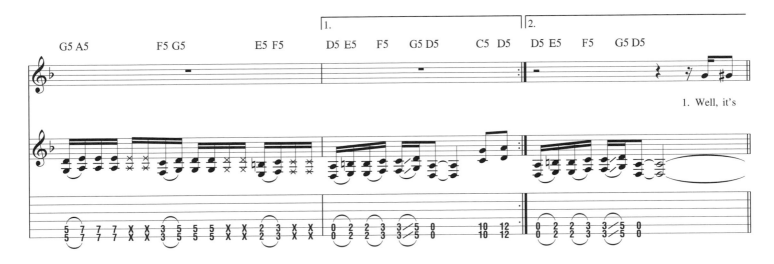

***Chord symbols reflect implied harmony.

Chorus

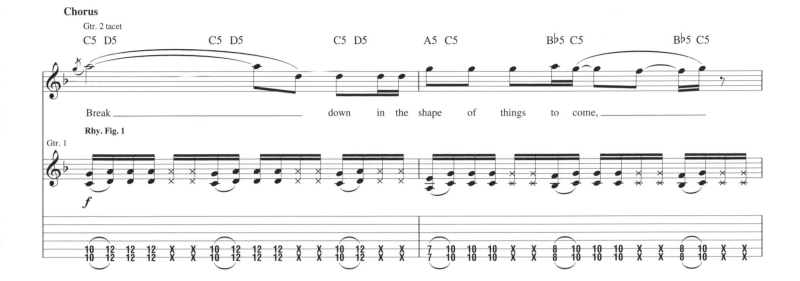

Gtr. 2 tacet

Break _____ down in the shape of things to come, _____

Rhy. Fig. 1
Gtr. 1

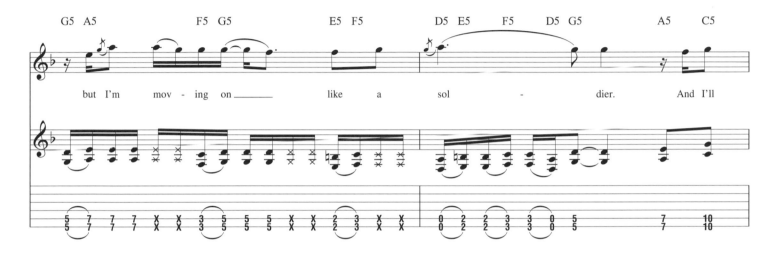

but I'm mov - ing on _____ like a sol - dier. And I'll

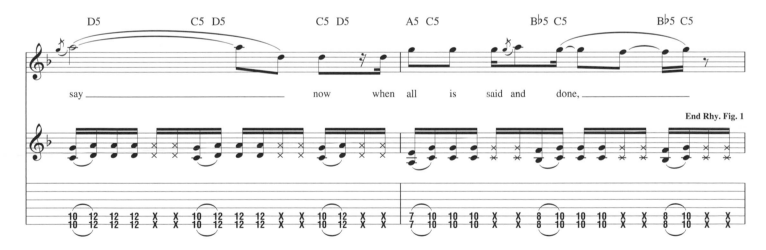

say _____ now when all is said and done, _____

End Rhy. Fig. 1

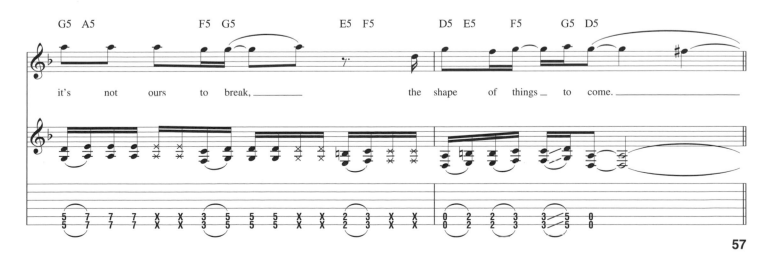

it's not ours to break, _____ the shape of things ___ to come. _____

Interlude

Verse

58

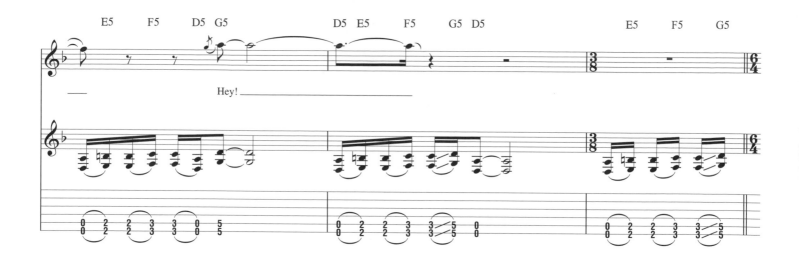

Bridge

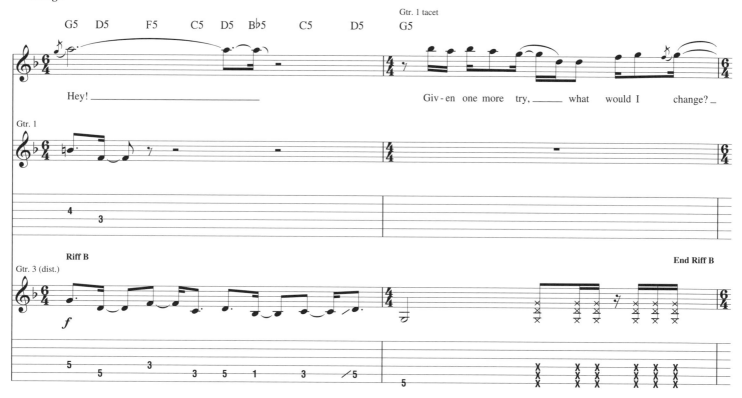

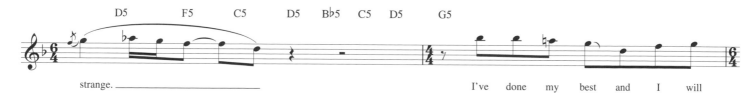

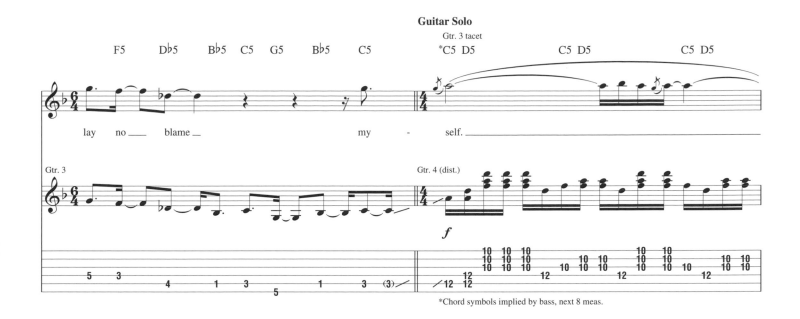

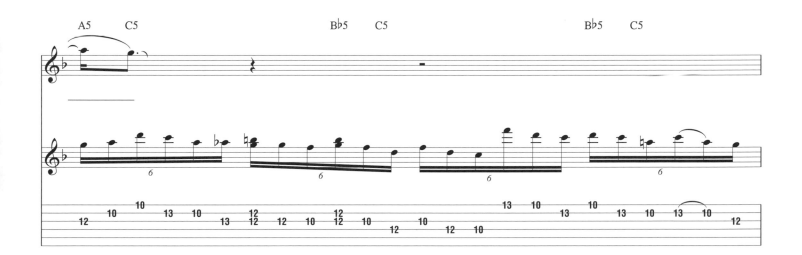

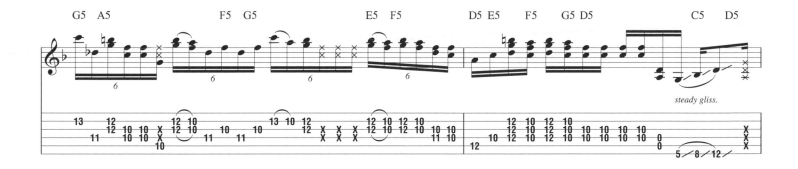

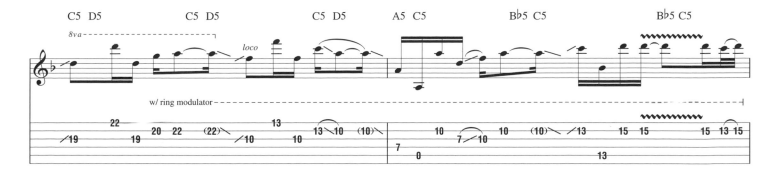

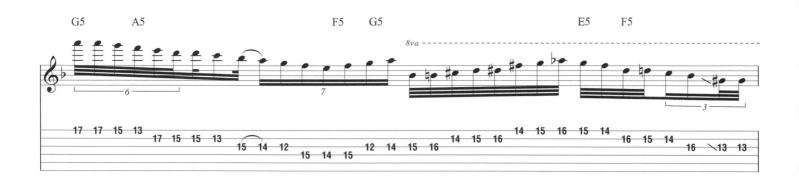

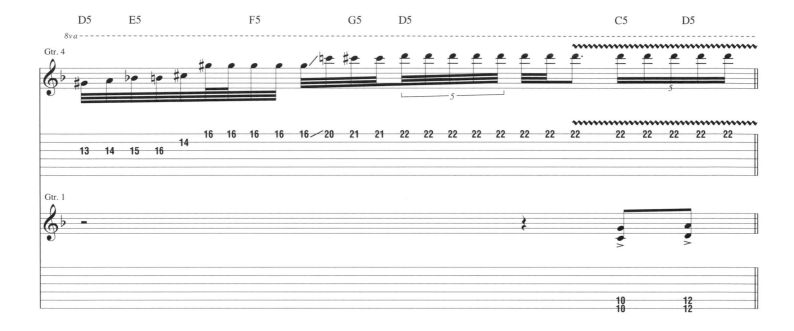

Chorus

Break _____ down _____ in the shape of things to come, _____

*Set for eighth-note regeneration w/ 5 repeats.

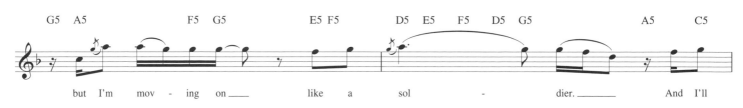

but I'm mov - ing on _____ like a sol - dier. _____ And I'll

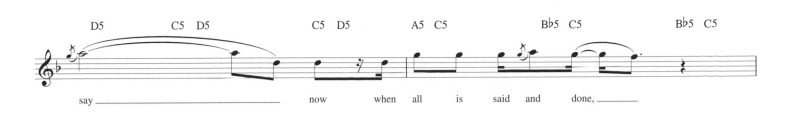

say _____ now when all is said and done, _____

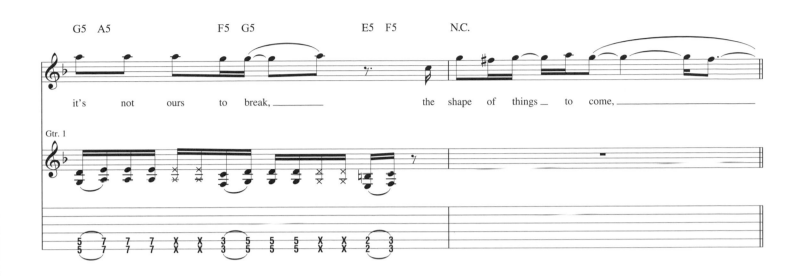

it's not ours to break, _____ the shape of things __ to come, _____

Outro

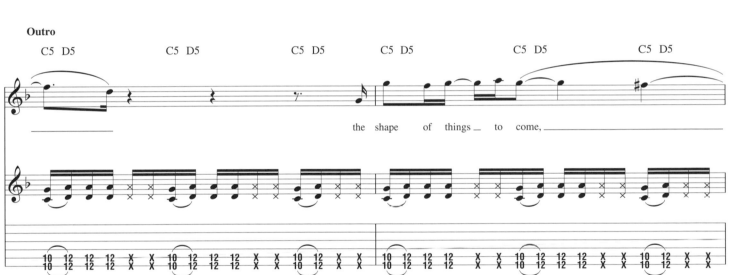

the shape of things __ to come, _____

_____ the shape of things __ to come. _____

Jewel of the Summertime

Lyrics by Chris Cornell
Music written and arranged by Audioslave

Drop D tuning:
(low to high) D-A-D-G-B-E

Intro

Moderately slow ♩ = 82

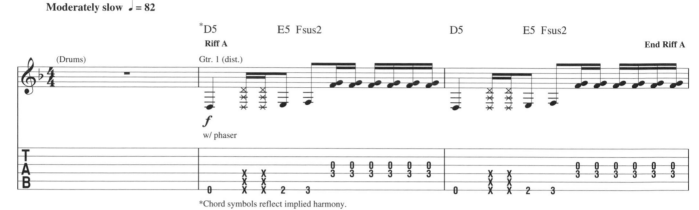

*Chord symbols reflect implied harmony.

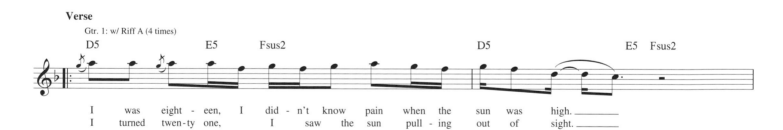

1. When

Verse

I was eight-teen, I did-n't know pain when the sun was high. ____
I turned twen-ty one, I saw the sun pull-ing out of sight. ____

Burnt face, shad-ows e-rased, and I knew I'd be ____ all right. ____ Left that be-
All that I met were dark sil-hou-ettes stumb-ling in ____ the night. ____ Then we col-

2nd time, Gtr. 2: w/ Rhy. Fill 1 (4 times)

D5   E5   Fsus2   D5   E5   Fsus2

hind me,   some-thing blind-ed me. _____ You're re-
lid-ed   and I fin-al-ly _____   got a
(Uh, huh.   Uh, huh.
(Uh, huh.   Uh, huh.

D5   E5   Fsus2   D5   E5   Fsus2

mind-ing me ____   of a bet-ter space __ in time, _____
light on me. ____   Now I'm bath-ing in _____ the bright _____ ul-tra-
Uh, huh.)
Uh, huh.)

Chorus

Asus2   F5   D5

miles _ a - way. _____   A jew-el of the sum-mer - time, ____

Gtr. 3 (dist.)   **Riff C**

                                mf

Gtrs. 1 & 2 (dist.)*   **Riff B

                                phaser off
                                **w/ wah-wah

*Composite arrangement   **Gtr. 2 only

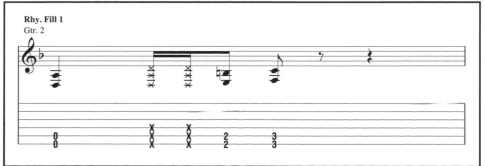

Rhy. Fill 1
Gtr. 2

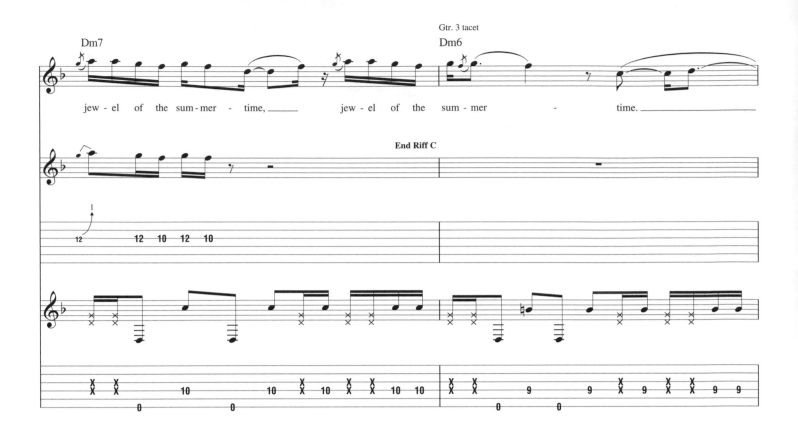

jew - el of the sum - mer - time, _____ jew - el of the sum - mer - time. _____

Gtr. 3 tacet

End Riff C

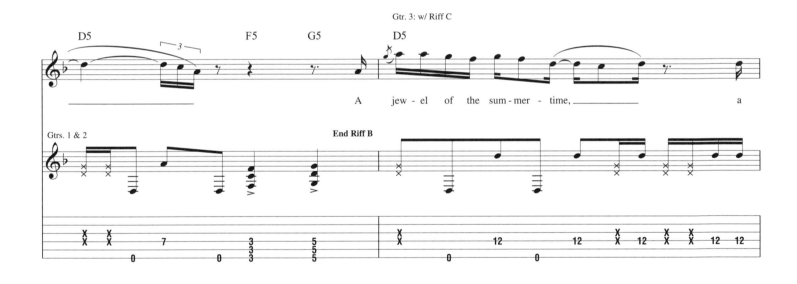

Gtr. 3: w/ Riff C

A jew - el of the sum - mer - time, _____ a

Gtrs. 1 & 2

End Riff B

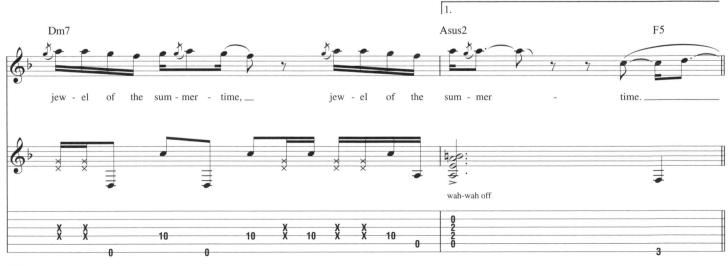

1.

jew - el of the sum - mer - time, _ jew - el of the sum - mer - time. _____

wah-wah off

Interlude

Gtr. 1: w/ Riff A (2 times)
Gtr. 2 tacet

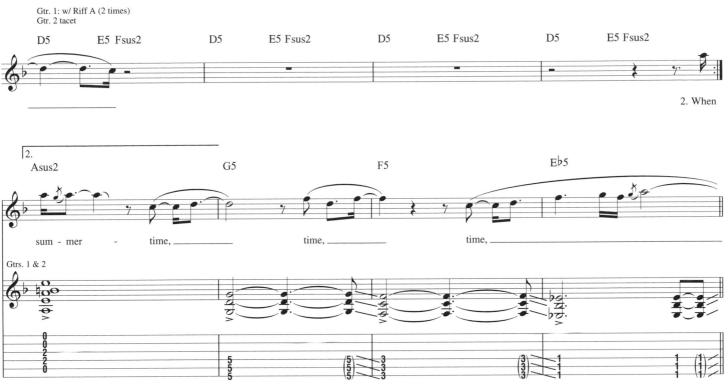

2. When

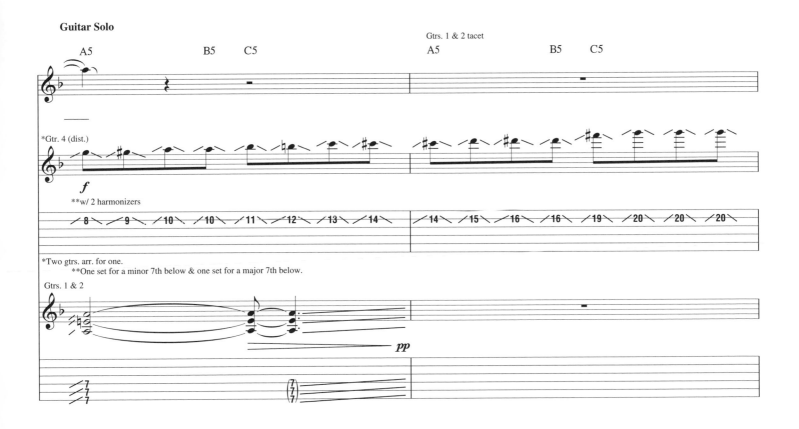

Guitar Solo

*Two gtrs. arr. for one.
**One set for a minor 7th below & one set for a major 7th below.

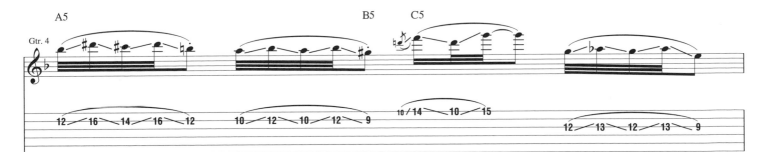

*Trem. pick in 32nd note pattern while sliding.
**Note fretted on pickup, causing muted sound.

**As before

Verse

Gtr. 1: w/ Riff A (2 times)
Gtr. 2: w/ Rhy. Fill 1 (4 times)
Gtr. 4 tacet

3. I left that be - hind me, some-thing blind - ed me. _____ You're re-
(Uh, huh. Uh, huh.

mind - ing me _____ of a bet - ter space _ in time, _____
Uh, huh.)

Chorus

Gtr. 2 tacet

miles _ a - way. _____ Jew - el of the sum - mer - time, _____

Gtrs. 1 & 2

Gtr. 1

phaser off

jew-el of the sum-mer - time, _ a jew-el of the sum-mer - time. _____ A

Gtrs. 1 & 2: w/ Riff B (3 times)
Gtr. 3: w/ Riff C

jew-el of the sum-mer - time, _____ jew-el of the sum-mer - time, _ a jew-el of the sum-mer - time. _

Gtr. 3: w/ Riff C

_____ A jew-el of the sum-mer - time, _____ jew-el of the sum-mer - time, _ jew-el of the

Gtr. 3: w/ Riff C

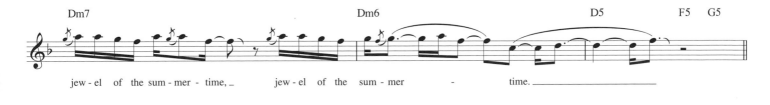

sum - mer - time. _____ Jew-el of the sum-mer - time, _____

jew-el of the sum-mer - time, _ jew-el of the sum - mer - time. _____

Outro   *Begin fade*   *Fade out*
Gtrs. 1 & 2: w/ Riff B (till fade)

Wide Awake

Lyrics by Chris Cornell
Music written and arranged by Audioslave

Drop D tuning:
(low to high) D-A-D-G-B-E

Intro

Moderately ♩ = 99

*Dm

Riff A

Gtrs. 1 & 2 (slight dist.)

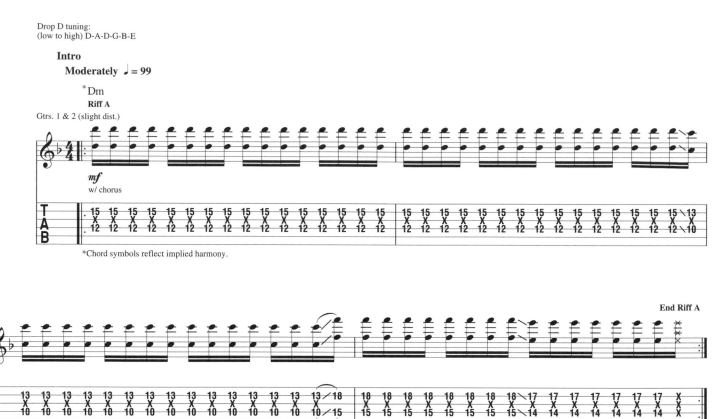

*Chord symbols reflect implied harmony.

Verse

Gtrs. 1 & 2: w/ Riff A (2 times)

Dm

1. You can look a hur - ri - cane___ right in the eye.

Twelve hun - dred peo - ple dead___ or left___ to die.

Fol - low the lead - ers. Were it an eye___

Riff B

Gtrs. 1 & 2

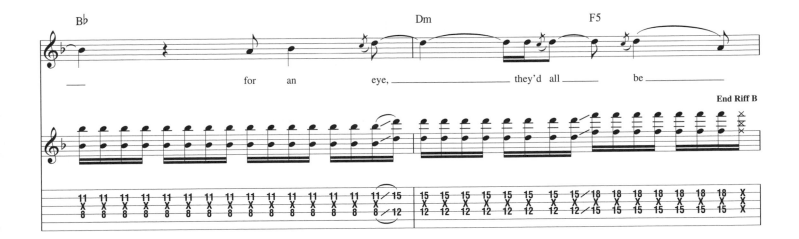

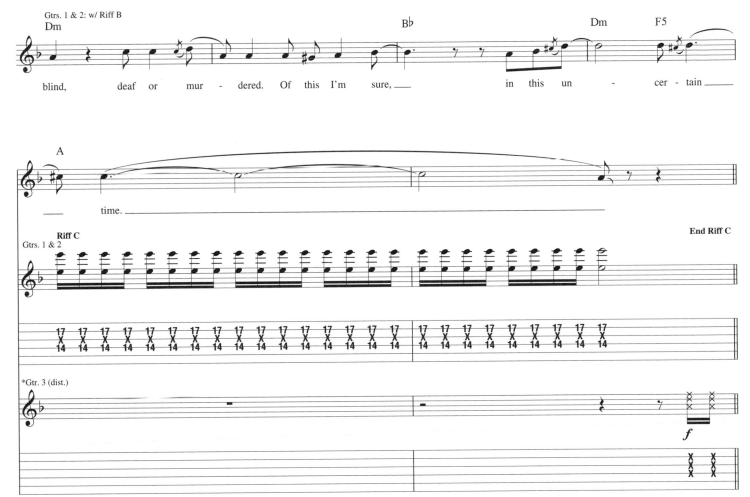

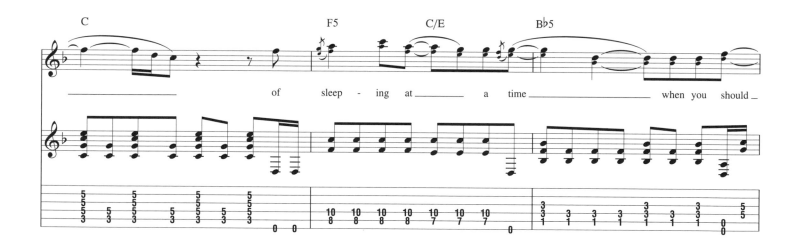

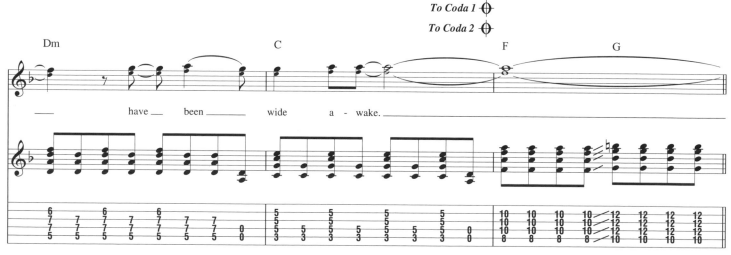

Interlude

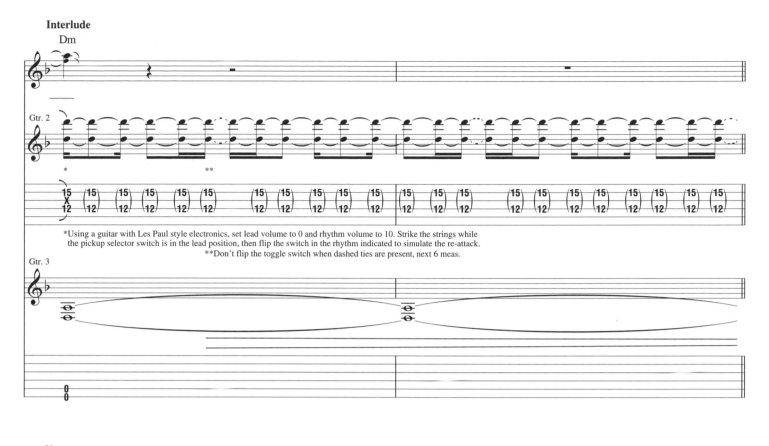

*Using a guitar with Les Paul style electronics, set lead volume to 0 and rhythm volume to 10. Strike the strings while
the pickup selector switch is in the lead position, then flip the switch in the rhythm indicated to simulate the re-attack.
**Don't flip the toggle switch when dashed ties are present, next 6 meas.

Verse

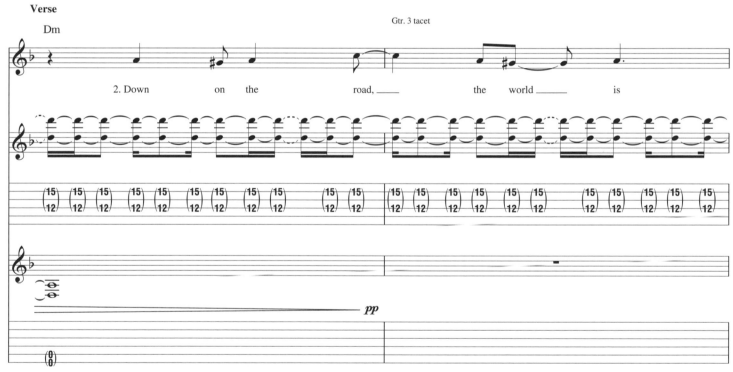

2. Down   on   the   road, ___   the   world ___   is

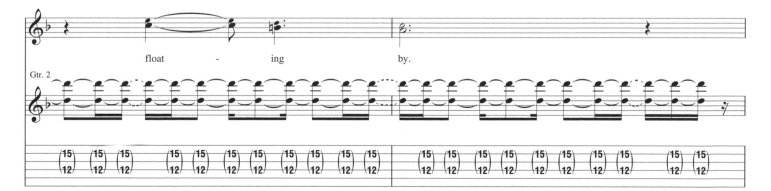

float   -   ing   by.

Gtrs. 1 & 2: w/ Riff A

The poor____ and un - de - fend - ed left ____ be -

Gtrs. 1 & 2: w/ Riff B

hind while you're some - where trad - ing lives ____ for oil, ____

D.S. al Coda 1

Gtrs. 1 & 2: w/ Riff C

Bb   Dm   F5   A

____ as if the whole ____ world ____ were ____ blind, _____ yeah. ____

Coda 1

Guitar Solo

Gtr. 3 tacet

F   G   Dm

Gtr. 3   **Riff D2**
                Gtr. 6

```
10  10  10  10 12  12    12    12
10  10  10  10 12  12    12    12
10  10  10  10 12  12    12    12
 8   8   8   8 10  10    10    10
```

```
7 /9 10 10/12    10  9    7 /9 10 10/12    10  9  (9)/
```

Gtrs. 5 & 6 (dist.)   **Riff D1**
                        Gtr. 5

𝆑

```
X   X   X      X   X   X
X   X   X      X   X   X
X   X   X      X   X   X
```

```
5 /7  8 8/10    8  7    5 /7  8 8/10    8  7  (7)/
```

Gtr. 4 (dist.)   **Riff D**

𝆑

```
X   X   X      X   X   X
X   X   X      X   X   X
X   X   X      X   X   X
```

```
0   2   3 3/5    3  2    0   2   3 3/5    3  2  (2)/
```

Chorus

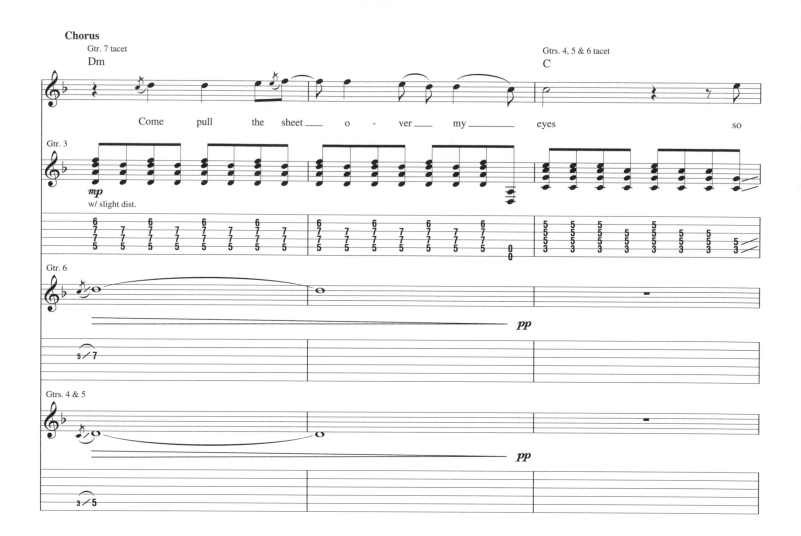

Come pull the sheet ___ o - ver ___ my ___ eyes ___ so

I ___ can sleep ___ to - night, _____ de - spite what I've _____

D.S.S. al Coda 2

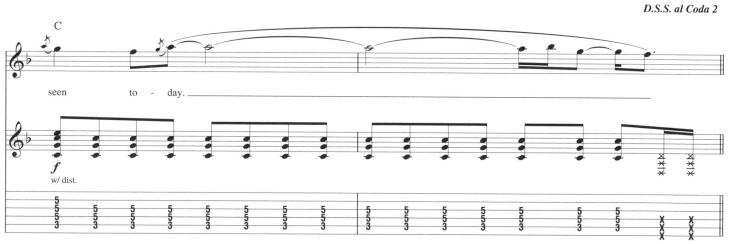

seen to - day. _____

76

⊕ Coda 2

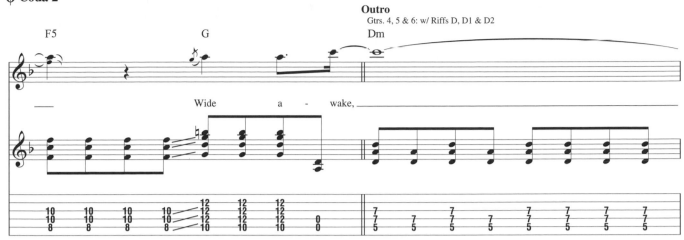

Nothing Left to Say but Goodbye

Lyrics by Chris Cornell
Music written and arranged by Audioslave

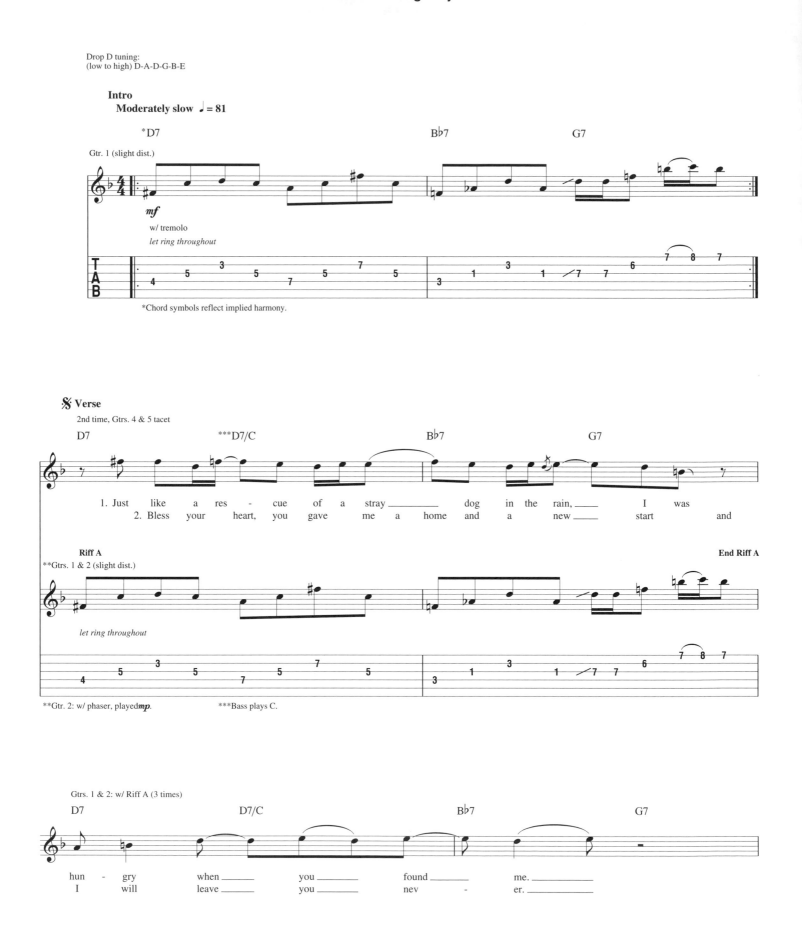

Verse

1. Just like a res - cue of a stray dog in the rain, I was
2. Bless your heart, you gave me a home and a new start and

hun - gry when you found me.
I will leave you nev - er.

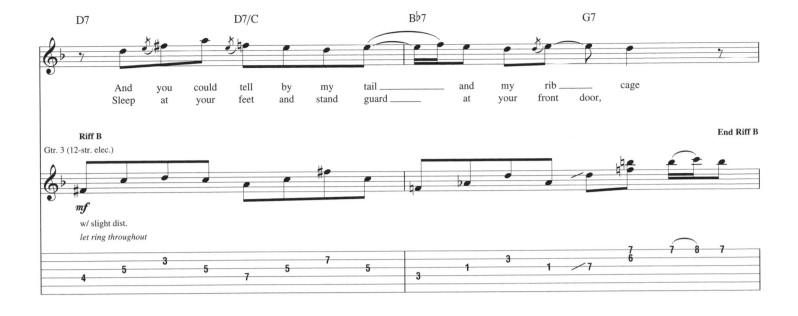

And   you   could   tell   by   my   tail _____ and   my   rib _____ cage
Sleep   at   your   feet   and   stand   guard _____ at   your   front   door,

To Coda ⊕

Chorus

what   was   once ___ a - round ___ me. _____   I   been   chased ___ by   a
I   will   keep ___ this   to - geth - er. _____

*Bass plays F.   **Gtr. 5 played *f*. Composite arrangement

rain ___ cloud. _____   I   was   lost _____ and   near - ly   drowned ___ and   kicked a - round, ___

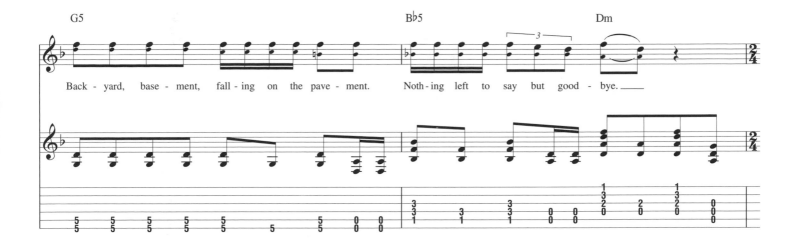

Back - yard, base - ment, fall - ing on the pave - ment. Noth - ing left to say but good - bye.

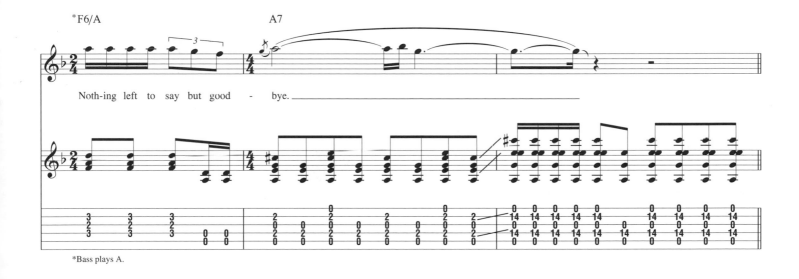

Noth - ing left to say but good - bye.

*Bass plays A.

Verse

Gtr. 4 tacet

3. It's true I ran a - way be - fore, but be sure

Riff C

Gtr. 1

End Riff C

tremolo off

P.M.

Gtr. 1: w/ Riff C (3 times)

Gtr. 3: w/ Riff B (2 times)

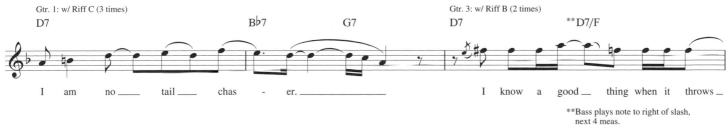

I am no ___ tail ___ chas - er. ___ I know a good ___ thing when it throws ___

**Bass plays note to right of slash, next 4 meas.

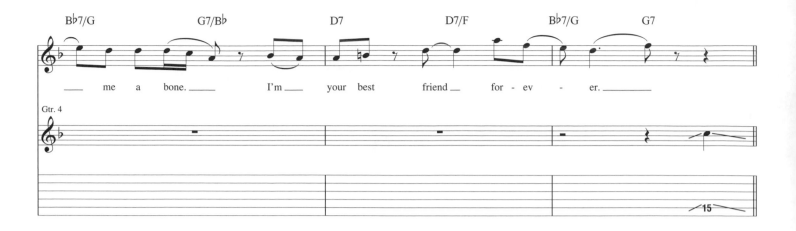

me a bone. ____ I'm ___ your best friend ___ for - ev - er. _____

Gtr. 4

Chorus

Gtrs. 4 & 5: w/ Rhy. Figs. 1 & 1A

I been chased ___ by a rain ___ cloud. _____ I was lost ___ and near - ly

drowned ___ and kicked a - round, ___ but now I'm ___ found _____ and I won't run a - way. __

Outro

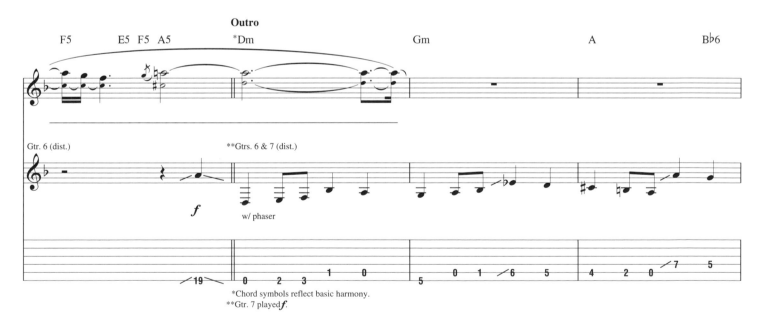

Gtr. 6 (dist.)

**Gtrs. 6 & 7 (dist.)

f

w/ phaser

*Chord symbols reflect basic harmony.
**Gtr. 7 played *f*.

Play 3 times & fade

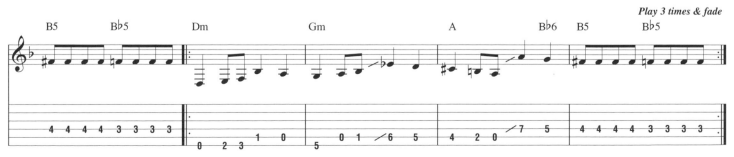

Moth

Lyrics by Chris Cornell
Music written and arranged by Audioslave

Drop D tuning:
(low to high) D-A-D-G-B-E

*First meas. located at 3:30 of track 11 on the CD.
**Chord symbols reflect overall harmony.
*** Delay set for eighth-note regeneration w/ 3 repeats.

†Doubled throughout

Verse

2nd time, Gtr. 2 tacet

1. Thought I was dif - fer - ent, _____ it seems I'm just the same. _____
2. I loved the heat, _____ I _____ loved the things that I for - got. _____

Gtr. 2

pp

Gtr. 3 (clean)

mf
*w/ delay

*Set for eighth-note regeneration w/ 1 repeat.

Gtr. 2 tacet

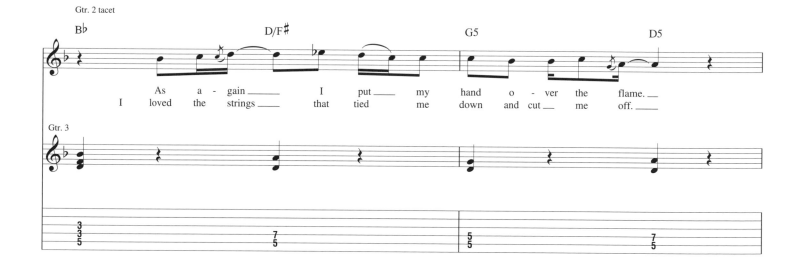

As a - gain _____ I put _____ my hand o - ver the flame. _____
I loved the strings _____ that tied me down and cut _____ me off. _____

Gtr. 3

I thought I was smart - er as _____ I flew in - to _____ the sun, _____
I was a king, _____ I was a moth _____ with paint - ed wings _____ made _____ of cloth. _____

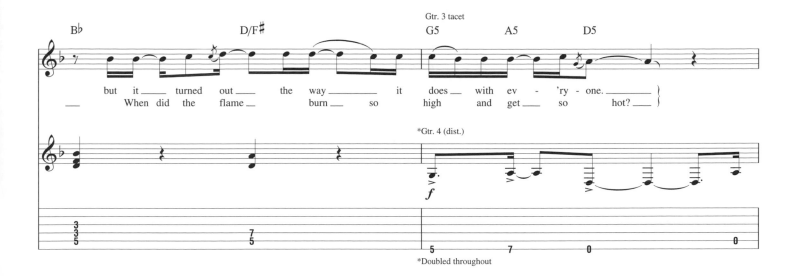

but it ___ turned out ___ the way ___ it does ___ with ev - 'ry - one. ___
When did the flame ___ burn ___ so high and get ___ so hot? ___

Oh, ___

oh. ___

𝄋 Chorus

1st time, Gtr. 2: w/ Riff A
Gtr. 4 tacet
2nd & 3rd times, Gtr. 2: w/ Riff A (1st 6 meas.)
3rd time, Gtr. 1 tacet

___ I don't fly a - round ___ your fire ___ an - y - more, ___ I don't fly a - round ___ your

**3rd time, voc. tacet on beat 1.

fire ___ an - y - more. ___ Burned and fall - en down ___ so man - y times ___ be - fore. ___

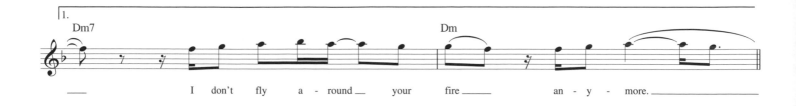

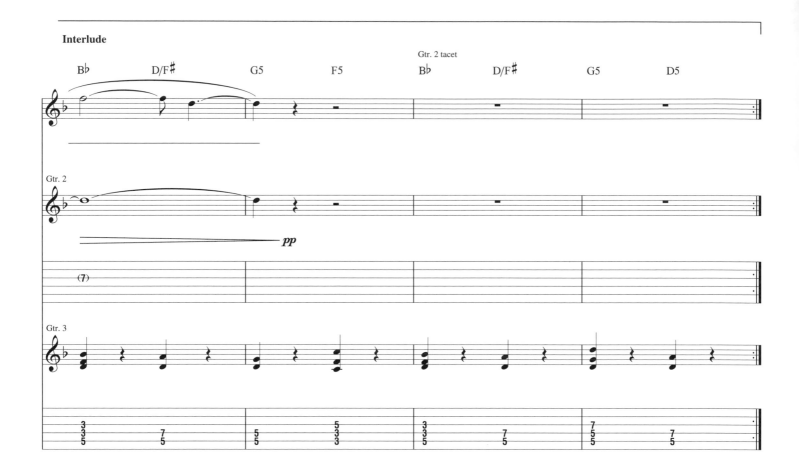

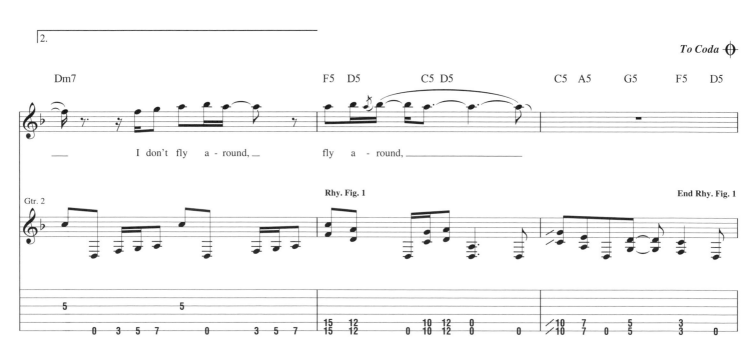

*Set for eighth-note regeneration w/ 3 repeats.

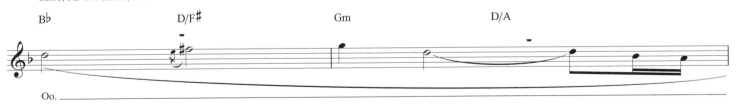

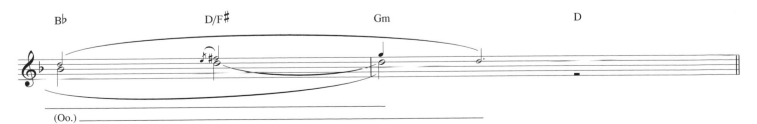

Bridge

Gtr. 1: w/ Rhy. Fig. 2 (1 1/2 times)

Gtr. 7

Gtr. 6

Gtr. 5
divisi

I don't fly a - round ___ your fire ___ an - y - more. _____ I don't fly a - round _____ your

Gtrs. 5, 6 & 7 tacet

fire ___ an - y - more. ___ Burned and fall - en down ___ so man - y times ___ be - fore. _____

D.S. al Coda
(take 2nd ending)

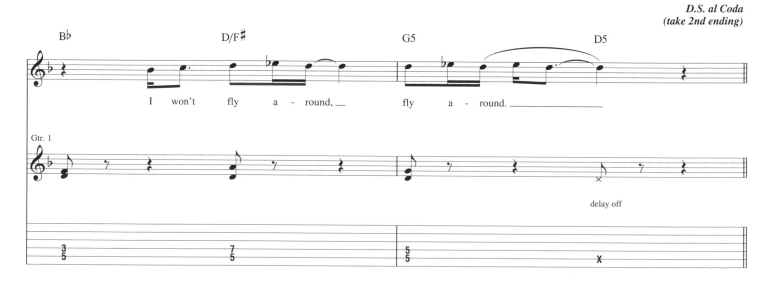

I won't fly a - round, ___ fly a - round. _____

Gtr. 1

delay off

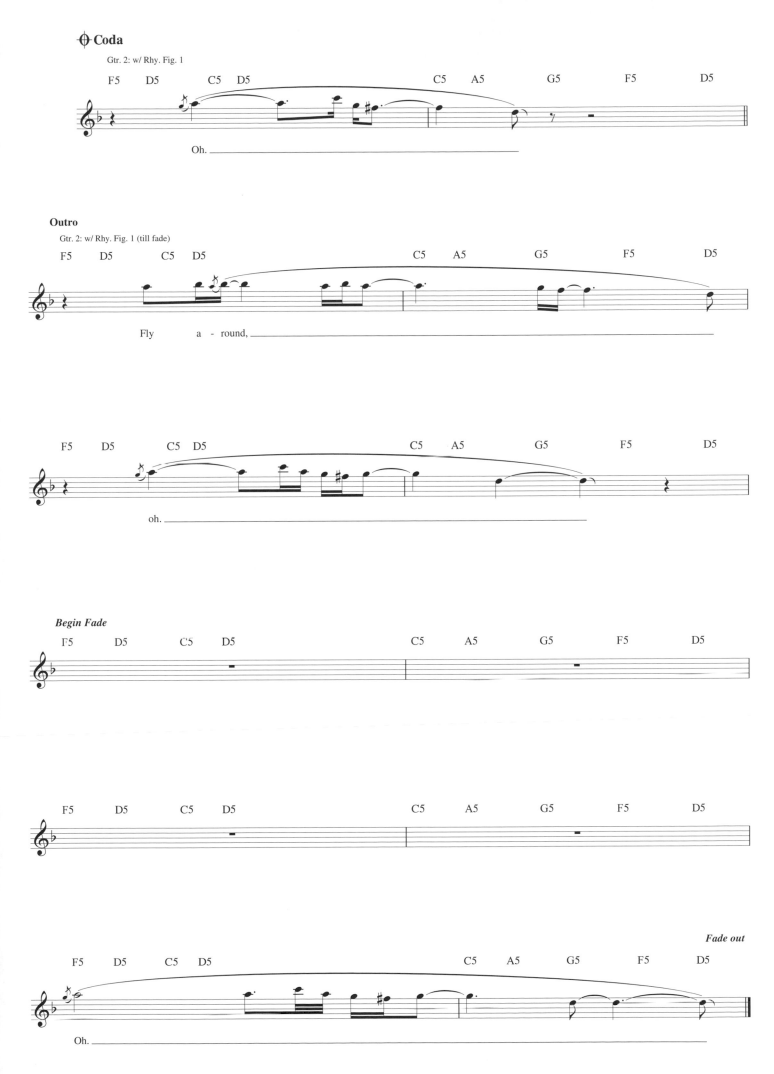

Guitar Notation Legend

Guitar music can be notated three different ways: on a *musical staff*, in *tablature*, and in *rhythm slashes*.

RHYTHM SLASHES are written above the staff. Strum chords in the rhythm indicated. Use the chord diagrams found at the top of the first page of the transcription for the appropriate chord voicings. Round noteheads indicate single notes.

THE MUSICAL STAFF shows pitches and rhythms and is divided by bar lines into measures. Pitches are named after the first seven letters of the alphabet.

TABLATURE graphically represents the guitar fingerboard. Each horizontal line represents a string, and each number represents a fret.

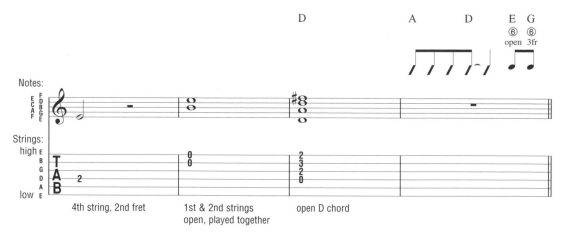

4th string, 2nd fret   1st & 2nd strings open, played together   open D chord

Definitions for Special Guitar Notation

HALF-STEP BEND: Strike the note and bend up 1/2 step.

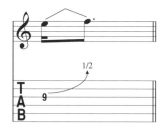

WHOLE-STEP BEND: Strike the note and bend up one step.

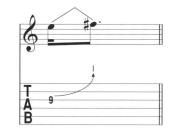

GRACE NOTE BEND: Strike the note and immediately bend up as indicated.

SLIGHT (MICROTONE) BEND: Strike the note and bend up 1/4 step.

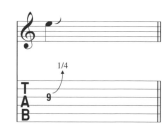

BEND AND RELEASE: Strike the note and bend up as indicated, then release back to the original note. Only the first note is struck.

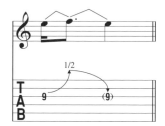

PRE-BEND: Bend the note as indicated, then strike it.

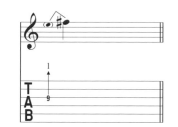

PRE-BEND AND RELEASE: Bend the note as indicated. Strike it and release the bend back to the original note.

UNISON BEND: Strike the two notes simultaneously and bend the lower note up to the pitch of the higher.

VIBRATO: The string is vibrated by rapidly bending and releasing the note with the fretting hand.

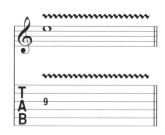

WIDE VIBRATO: The pitch is varied to a greater degree by vibrating with the fretting hand.

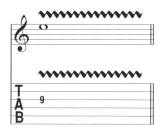

HAMMER-ON: Strike the first (lower) note with one finger, then sound the higher note (on the same string) with another finger by fretting it without picking.

PULL-OFF: Place both fingers on the notes to be sounded. Strike the first note and without picking, pull the finger off to sound the second (lower) note.

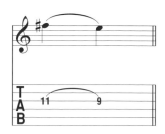

LEGATO SLIDE: Strike the first note and then slide the same fret-hand finger up or down to the second note. The second note is not struck.

SHIFT SLIDE: Same as legato slide, except the second note is struck.

TRILL: Very rapidly alternate between the notes indicated by continuously hammering on and pulling off.

TAPPING: Hammer ("tap") the fret indicated with the pick-hand index or middle finger and pull off to the note fretted by the fret hand.

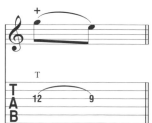

NATURAL HARMONIC: Strike the note while the fret-hand lightly touches the string directly over the fret indicated.

PINCH HARMONIC: The note is fretted normally and a harmonic is produced by adding the edge of the thumb or the tip of the index finger of the pick hand to the normal pick attack.

HARP HARMONIC: The note is fretted normally and a harmonic is produced by gently resting the pick hand's index finger directly above the indicated fret (in parentheses) while the pick hand's thumb or pick assists by plucking the appropriate string.

PICK SCRAPE: The edge of the pick is rubbed down (or up) the string, producing a scratchy sound.

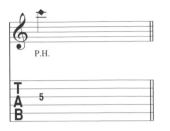

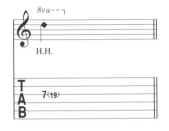

MUFFLED STRINGS: A percussive sound is produced by laying the fret hand across the string(s) without depressing, and striking them with the pick hand.

PALM MUTING: The note is partially muted by the pick hand lightly touching the string(s) just before the bridge.

RAKE: Drag the pick across the strings indicated with a single motion.

TREMOLO PICKING: The note is picked as rapidly and continuously as possible.

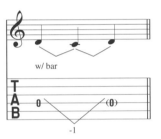

ARPEGGIATE: Play the notes of the chord indicated by quickly rolling them from bottom to top.

VIBRATO BAR DIVE AND RETURN: The pitch of the note or chord is dropped a specified number of steps (in rhythm), then returned to the original pitch.

VIBRATO BAR SCOOP: Depress the bar just before striking the note, then quickly release the bar.

VIBRATO BAR DIP: Strike the note and then immediately drop a specified number of steps, then release back to the original pitch.

Additional Musical Definitions

(accent)	• Accentuate note (play it louder).	
(accent)	• Accentuate note with great intensity.	
(staccato)	• Play the note short.	
	• Downstroke	
V	• Upstroke	
D.S. al Coda	• Go back to the sign (𝄋), then play until the measure marked "*To Coda*," then skip to the section labelled "**Coda**."	
D.C. al Fine	• Go back to the beginning of the song and play until the measure marked "*Fine*" (end).	

Rhy. Fig. — • Label used to recall a recurring accompaniment pattern (usually chordal).

Riff — • Label used to recall composed, melodic lines (usually single notes) which recur.

Fill — • Label used to identify a brief melodic figure which is to be inserted into the arrangement.

Rhy. Fill — • A chordal version of a Fill.

tacet — • Instrument is silent (drops out).

• Repeat measures between signs.

• When a repeated section has different endings, play the first ending only the first time and the second ending only the second time.

NOTE: Tablature numbers in parentheses mean:
    1. The note is being sustained over a system (note in standard notation is tied), or
    2. The note is sustained, but a new articulation (such as a hammer-on, pull-off, slide or vibrato) begins, or
    3. The note is a barely audible "ghost" note (note in standard notation is also in parentheses).

RECORDED VERSIONS GUITAR

AUTHENTIC TRANSCRIPTIONS WITH NOTES AND TABLATURE

GUITAR RECORDED VERSIONS®

Guitar Recorded Versions® are note-for-note transcriptions of guitar music taken directly off recordings. This series, one of the most popular in print today, features some of the greatest guitar players and groups from blues and rock to country and jazz.

Guitar Recorded Versions are transcribed by the best transcribers in the business. Every book contains notes and tablature.

00690016	Will Ackerman Collection	$19.95
00690501	Bryan Adams – Greatest Hits	$19.95
00690002	Aerosmith – Big Ones	$24.95
00692015	Aerosmith – Greatest Hits	$22.95
00690603	Aerosmith – O Yeah! (Ultimate Hits)	$24.95
00690147	Aerosmith – Rocks	$19.95
00690146	Aerosmith – Toys in the Attic	$19.95
00690139	Alice in Chains	$19.95
00690178	Alice in Chains – Acoustic	$19.95
00694865	Alice in Chains – Dirt	$19.95
00660225	Alice in Chains – Facelift	$19.95
00694925	Alice in Chains – Jar of Flies/Sap	$19.95
00690387	Alice in Chains – Nothing Safe: Best of the Box	$19.95
00690812	All American Rejects – Move Along	$19.95
00694932	Allman Brothers Band – Definitive Collection for Guitar Volume 1	$24.95
00694933	Allman Brothers Band – Definitive Collection for Guitar Volume 2	$24.95
00694934	Allman Brothers Band – Definitive Collection for Guitar Volume 3	$24.95
00690755	Alter Bridge – One Day Remains	$19.95
00690571	Trey Anastasio	$19.95
00690158	Chet Atkins – Almost Alone	$19.95
00694876	Chet Atkins – Contemporary Styles	$19.95
00694878	Chet Atkins – Vintage Fingerstyle	$19.95
00690418	Best of Audio Adrenaline	$17.95
00690609	Audioslave	$19.95
00690804	Audioslave – Out of Exile	$19.95
00694918	Randy Bachman Collection	$22.95
00690366	Bad Company – Original Anthology – Book 1	$19.95
00690367	Bad Company – Original Anthology – Book 2	$19.95
00690503	Beach Boys – Very Best of	$19.95
00694929	Beatles: 1962-1966	$24.95
00694930	Beatles: 1967-1970	$24.95
00690489	Beatles – 1	$24.95
00694880	Beatles – Abbey Road	$19.95
00690110	Beatles – Book 1 (White Album)	$19.95
00690111	Beatles – Book 2 (White Album)	$19.95
00694832	Beatles – For Acoustic Guitar	$22.95
00690137	Beatles – A Hard Day's Night	$16.95
00690482	Beatles – Let It Be	$16.95
00694891	Beatles – Revolver	$19.95
00694914	Beatles – Rubber Soul	$19.95
00694863	Beatles – Sgt. Pepper's Lonely Hearts Club Band	$19.95
00690383	Beatles – Yellow Submarine	$19.95
00690792	Beck – Guero	$19.95
00690175	Beck – Odelay	$17.95
00690346	Beck – Mutations	$19.95
00690632	Beck – Sea Change	$19.95
00694884	Best of George Benson	$19.95
00692385	Chuck Berry	$19.95
00690149	Black Sabbath	$14.95
00690148	Black Sabbath – Master of Reality	$14.95
00690142	Black Sabbath – Paranoid	$14.95
00692200	Black Sabbath – We Sold Our Soul for Rock 'N' Roll	$19.95
00690115	Blind Melon – Soup	$19.95
00690674	Blink-182	$19.95
00690305	Blink-182 – Dude Ranch	$19.95
00690389	Blink-182 – Enema of the State	$19.95
00690523	Blink-182 – Take Off Your Pants and Jacket	$19.95
00690028	Blue Oyster Cult – Cult Classics	$19.95
00690008	Bon Jovi – Cross Road	$19.95
00690491	Best of David Bowie	$19.95
00690583	Box Car Racer	$19.95
00690764	Breaking Benjamin – We Are Not Alone	$19.95
00690451	Jeff Buckley Collection	$24.95
00690364	Cake – Songbook	$19.95
00690564	The Calling – Camino Palmero	$19.95
00690261	Carter Family Collection	$19.95
00690293	Best of Steven Curtis Chapman	$19.95
00690043	Best of Cheap Trick	$19.95
00690171	Chicago – The Definitive Guitar Collection	$22.95
00690567	Charlie Christian – The Definitive Collection	$19.95
00690590	Eric Clapton – Anthology	$29.95
00692391	Best of Eric Clapton – 2nd Edition	$22.95
00690393	Eric Clapton – Selections from Blues	$19.95
00690074	Eric Clapton – Cream of Clapton	$24.95
00690265	Eric Clapton – E.C. Was Here	$19.95
00690010	Eric Clapton – From the Cradle	$19.95
00690716	Eric Clapton – Me and Mr. Johnson	$19.95
00690263	Eric Clapton – Slowhand	$19.95
00694873	Eric Clapton – Timepieces	$19.95
00694869	Eric Clapton – Unplugged	$22.95
00690415	Clapton Chronicles – Best of Eric Clapton	$18.95
00694896	John Mayall/Eric Clapton – Bluesbreakers	$19.95
00690162	Best of The Clash	$19.95
00690682	Coldplay – Live in 2003	$19.95
00690494	Coldplay – Parachutes	$19.95
00690593	Coldplay – A Rush of Blood to the Head	$19.95
00690806	Coldplay – X & Y	$19.95
00694940	Counting Crows – August & Everything After	$19.95
00690197	Counting Crows – Recovering the Satellites	$19.95
00690405	Counting Crows – This Desert Life	$19.95
00694840	Cream – Disraeli Gears	$19.95
00690285	Cream – Those Were the Days	$17.95
00690401	Creed – Human Clay	$19.95
00690352	Creed – My Own Prison	$19.95
00690551	Creed – Weathered	$19.95
00690648	Very Best of Jim Croce	$19.95
00690572	Steve Cropper – Soul Man	$19.95
00690613	Best of Crosby, Stills & Nash	$19.95
00690777	Crossfade	$19.95
00699521	The Cure – Greatest Hits	$24.95
00690637	Best of Dick Dale	$19.95
00690184	dc Talk – Jesus Freak	$19.95
00690289	Best of Deep Purple	$17.95
00694831	Derek and The Dominos – Layla & Other Assorted Love Songs	$19.95
00690384	Best of Ani DiFranco	$19.95
00690322	Ani DiFranco – Little Plastic Castle	$19.95
00690380	Ani DiFranco – Up Up Up Up Up Up	$19.95
00690191	Dire Straits – Money for Nothing	$24.95
00695382	Very Best of Dire Straits – Sultans of Swing	$19.95
00660178	Willie Dixon – Master Blues Composer	$24.95
00690347	The Doors – Anthology	$22.95
00690348	The Doors – Essential Guitar Collection	$16.95
00690250	Best of Duane Eddy	$16.95
00690533	Electric Light Orchestra Guitar Collection	$19.95
00690555	Best of Melissa Etheridge	$19.95
00690524	Melissa Etheridge – Skin	$19.95
00690496	Best of Everclear	$19.95
00690515	Extreme II – Pornograffitti	$19.95
00690810	Fall Out Boy – From Under the Cork Tree	$19.95
00690664	Best of Fleetwood Mac	$19.95
00690734	Franz Ferdinand	$19.95
00694920	Best of Free	$19.95
00690257	John Fogerty – Blue Moon Swamp	$19.95
00690089	Foo Fighters	$19.95
00690235	Foo Fighters – The Colour and the Shape	$19.95
00690808	Foo Fighters – In Your Honor	$19.95
00690595	Foo Fighters – One by One	$19.95
00690394	Foo Fighters – There Is Nothing Left to Lose	$19.95
00690222	G3 Live – Joe Satriani, Steve Vai, and Eric Johnson	$22.95
00694807	Danny Gatton – 88 Elmira St	$19.95
00690438	Genesis Guitar Anthology	$19.95
00120167	Godsmack	$19.95
00690753	Best of Godsmack	$19.95
00690127	Goo Goo Dolls – A Boy Named Goo	$19.95
00690338	Goo Goo Dolls – Dizzy Up the Girl	$19.95
00690576	Goo Goo Dolls – Gutterflower	$19.95
00690773	Good Charlotte – Chronicles of Life and Death	$19.95
00690601	Good Charlotte – The Young and the Hopeless	$19.95
00690117	John Gorka Collection	$19.95
00690591	Patty Griffin – Guitar Collection	$19.95
00690114	Buddy Guy Collection Vol. A-J	$22.95
00690193	Buddy Guy Collection Vol. L-Y	$22.95
00690697	Best of Jim Hall	$19.95
00694798	George Harrison Anthology	$19.95
00690778	Hawk Nelson – Letters to the President	$19.95
00690068	Return of the Hellecasters	$19.95
00692930	Jimi Hendrix – Are You Experienced?	$24.95
00692931	Jimi Hendrix – Axis: Bold As Love	$22.95
00690304	Jimi Hendrix – Band of Gypsys	$19.95
00690321	Jimi Hendrix – BBC Sessions	$22.95
00690608	Jimi Hendrix – Blue Wild Angel	$24.95
00694944	Jimi Hendrix – Blues	$24.95
00692932	Jimi Hendrix – Electric Ladyland	$24.95
00690218	Jimi Hendrix – First Rays of the Rising Sun	$27.95
00660099	Jimi Hendrix – Radio One	$24.95
00690280	Jimi Hendrix – South Saturn Delta	$24.95
00690602	Jimi Hendrix – Smash Hits	$19.95
00690017	Jimi Hendrix – Woodstock	$24.95
00660029	Buddy Holly	$19.95
00660169	John Lee Hooker – A Blues Legend	$19.95
00694905	Howlin' Wolf	$19.95
00690692	Very Best of Billy Idol	$19.95
00690688	Incubus – A Crow Left of the Murder	$19.95
00690457	Incubus – Make Yourself	$19.95
00690544	Incubus – Morningview	$19.95
00690136	Indigo Girls – 1200 Curfews	$22.95
00690730	Alan Jackson – Guitar Collection	$19.95
00694938	Elmore James – Master Electric Slide Guitar	$19.95
00690652	Best of Jane's Addiction	$19.95
00690721	Jet – Get Born	$19.95
00690684	Jethro Tull – Aqualung	$19.95
00690647	Best of Jewel	$19.95
00694833	Billy Joel for Guitar	$19.95
00690751	John5 – Vertigo	$19.95
00660147	Eric Johnson	$19.95
00694912	Eric Johnson – Ah Via Musicom	$19.95
00690660	Best of Eric Johnson	$19.95
00690169	Eric Johnson – Venus Isle	$22.95
00690271	Robert Johnson – The New Transcriptions	$24.95
00699131	Best of Janis Joplin	$19.95
00690427	Best of Judas Priest	$19.95
00690651	Juanes – Exitos de Juanes	$19.95
00690277	Best of Kansas	$19.95
00690742	The Killers – Hot Fuss	$19.95
00690504	Very Best of Albert King	$19.95
00690073	B. B. King – 1950-1957	$24.95
00690444	B.B. King & Eric Clapton – Riding with the King	$19.95
00690134	Freddie King Collection	$19.95
00690339	Best of the Kinks	$19.95
00690156	Kiss	$17.95
00690157	Kiss – Alive!	$19.95
00694903	Best of Kiss for Guitar	$24.95
00690188	Mark Knopfler – Golden Heart	$19.95
00690164	Mark Knopfler Guitar – Vol. 1	$19.95
00690165	Mark Knopfler Guitar – Vol. 2	$19.95
00690163	Mark Knopfler/Chet Atkins – Neck and Neck	$19.95
00690780	Korn – Greatest Hits, Volume 1	$22.95
00690377	Kris Kristofferson Collection	$17.95
00690658	Johnny Lang – Long Time Coming	$19.95
00690614	Avril Lavigne – Let Go	$19.95
00690726	Avril Lavigne – Under My Skin	$19.95
00690679	John Lennon – Guitar Collection	$19.95
00690279	Ottmar Liebert + Luna Negra – Opium Highlights	$19.95
00690785	Best of Limp Bizkit	$19.95
00690781	Linkin Park – Hybrid Theory	$22.95
00690782	Linkin Park – Meteora	$22.95
00690783	Best of Live	$19.95
00699623	Best of Chuck Loeb	$19.95
00690743	Los Lonely Boys	$19.95
00690720	Lostprophets – Start Something	$19.95
00690525	Best of George Lynch	$19.95
00694954	New Best of Lynyrd Skynyrd	$19.95
00690577	Yngwie Malmsteen – Anthology	$24.95
00694845	Yngwie Malmsteen – Fire and Ice	$19.95
00694755	Yngwie Malmsteen's Rising Force	$19.95

THE DECADE SERIES

These Guitar Recorded Versions collections feature the top tunes that shaped a decade, transcribed note-for-note with tab.

The 1950s

35 pivotal songs from the early rock years: All Shook Up • Donna • Heartbreak Hotel • Hound Dog • I'm Movin' On • Lonesome Town • Matchbox • Moonlight in Vermont • My Babe • Poor Little Fool • Race With the Devil • Rebel 'Rouser • Rock Around the Clock • Rockin' Robin • Sleepwalk • Slippin' and Slidin' • Sweet Little Angel • Tequila • Wake Up Little Susie • Yankee Doodle Dixie • and more.

00690543................................$15.95

The 1960s

30 songs that defined the '60s: Badge • Blackbird • Fun, Fun, Fun • Gloria • Good Lovin' • Happy Together • Hey Joe • Hush • I Can See for Miles • I Feel Fine • I Get Around • Louie, Louie • My Girl • Oh, Pretty Woman • On the Road Again • Somebody to Love • Soul Man • Suite: Judy Blue Eyes • Susie-Q • Wild Thing • and more.

00690542................................$15.95

The 1970s

30 top songs from the '70s: Best of My Love • Breakdown • Dust in the Wind • Evil Woman • Landslide • Lay Down Sally • Let It Be • Maggie May • No Woman No Cry • Oye Como Va • Show Me the Way • Smoke on the Water • So Into You • Space Oddity • Stayin' Alive • Teach Your Children • Time in a Bottle • Walk This Way • Wheel in the Sky • You've Got a Friend • and more.

00690541................................$16.95

The 1980s

30 songs that best represent the decade: 867-5309/Jenny • Every Breath You Take • Eye of the Tiger • Fight for Your Right (To Party) • Heart and Soul • Hit Me With Your Best Shot • I Love Rock 'N Roll • La Bamba • Money for Nothing • Mony, Mony • Refugee • Rock Me • Rock You Like a Hurricane • Start Me Up • Summer of '69 • Sweet Child O' Mine • Wait • What I Like About You • and more.

00690540................................$16.95

The 1990s

30 essential '90s classics: All I Wanna Do • Barely Breathing • Building a Mystery • Come Out and Play • Cryin' • Fields of Gold • Friends in Low Places • Hold My Hand • I Can't Dance • Iris • Jump, Jive an' Wail • More Than Words • Santa Monica • Semi-Charmed Life • Silent Lucidity • Smells Like Teen Spirit • Smooth • Tears in Heaven • Two Princes • Under the Bridge • Wonderwall • and more.

00690539................................$16.95

The 2000s

30 songs, including: Alive • All the Small Things • Are You Gonna Be My Girl • Californication • Click Click Boom • Complicated • Drive • Hanging by a Moment • Heaven • If You're Gone • Kryptonite • Lifestyles of the Rich and Famous • Maps • The Space Between • Take a Look Around (Theme from *M:I-2*) • Wherever You Will Go • Yellow • and more.

00690761................................$15.95

More of the 1950s

30 top songs of the '50s, including: Blue Suede Shoes • Bye Bye Love • Don't Be Cruel (To a Heart That's True) • Hard Headed Woman • Jailhouse Rock • La Bamba • Peggy Sue • Rawhide • Say Man • See You Later, Alligator • That'll Be the Day • Yakety Yak • and more.

00690756................................$14.95

More of the 1960s

30 great songs of the '60s: All Along the Watchtower • Born to Be Wild • Brown Eyed Girl • California Dreamin' • Do You Believe in Magic • Hang On Sloopy • I'm a Believer • Paperback Writer • Secret Agent Man • So You Want to Be a Rock and Roll Star • Sunshine of Your Love • Surfin' U.S.A. • Ticket to Ride • Travelin' Man • White Rabbit • With a Little Help from My Friends • and more.

00690757................................$14.95

More of the 1970s

30 more hits from the '70s: Aqualung • Carry on Wayward Son • Evil Ways • Feel like Makin' Love • Fly like an Eagle • Give a Little Bit • I Want You to Want Me • Lights • My Sharona • One Way or Another • Rock and Roll All Nite • Roxanne • Saturday Night's Alright (For Fighting) • Suffragette City • Sultans of Swing • Sweet Emotion • Sweet Home Alabama • Won't Get Fooled Again • Wonderful Tonight • and more.

00690758................................$17.95

More of the 1980s

30 songs that defined the decade: Call Me • Crazy Crazy Nights • Heartbreaker • Here I Go Again • It's Still Rock and Roll to Me • Jack and Diane • Jessie's Girl • Once Bitten Twice Shy • Rock the Casbah • Runnin' Down a Dream • Sharp Dressed Man • Smokin' in the Boys Room • Stray Cat Strut • Wanted Dead or Alive • White Wedding • and more.

00690759................................$16.95

More of the 1990s

30 songs: Alive • Change the World • Come as You Are • The Freshmen • Hard to Handle • Hole Hearted • Just a Girl • Lightning Crashes • Mr. Jones • No Excuses • No Rain • Only Wanna Be with You • Pretty Fly (For a White Guy) • Push • Shimmer • Stay • Stupid Girl • What I Got • Whatever • Whiskey in the Jar • Zombie • and more.

00690760................................$14.95

More of the 2000s

30 recent hits: All Downhill From Here • By the Way • Clocks • Cold Hard Bitch • Drops of Jupiter (Tell Me) • Harder to Breathe • I Did It • I Hate Everything About You • Learn to Fly • Ocean Avenue • St. Anger • Wasting My Time • When I'm Gone • Wish You Were Here • With Arms Wide Open • Youth of the Nation • and more.

00690762................................$16.95

Prices, contents and availability subject to change without notice.

FOR MORE INFORMATION, SEE YOUR LOCAL MUSIC DEALER, OR WRITE TO:

HAL•LEONARD® CORPORATION

7777 W. BLUEMOUND RD. P.O. BOX 13819 MILWAUKEE, WI 53213

Complete songlists available online at
www.halleonard.com

0706

GUITAR BIBLES

from HAL•LEONARD®

Hal Leonard proudly presents the Guitar Bible series. Each volume contains great songs in authentic, note-for-note transcriptions with lyrics and tablature.

ACOUSTIC GUITAR BIBLE
35 acoustic classics: Angie • Building a Mystery • Change the World • Dust in the Wind • Hold My Hand • Iris • Maggie May • Southern Cross • Tears in Heaven • Wild World • and more.
00690432...$19.95

ACOUSTIC ROCK GUITAR BIBLE
35 classics: And I Love Her • Behind Blue Eyes • Come to My Window • Free Fallin' • Give a Little Bit • More Than Words • Night Moves • Pink Houses • Slide • 3 AM • and more.
00690625...$19.95

BABY BOOMER'S GUITAR BIBLE
35 songs: Angie • Can't Buy Me Love • Happy Together • Hey Jude • Imagine • Laughing • Longer • My Girl • New Kid in Town • Rebel, Rebel • Wild Thing • and more.
00690412...$19.95

BLUES GUITAR BIBLE
35 blues tunes: Boom Boom • Hide Away • I Can't Quit You Baby • I'm Your Hoochie Coochie Man • Killing Floor • Pride and Joy • Sweet Little Angel • The Thrill Is Gone • and more.
00690437...$19.95

BLUES-ROCK GUITAR BIBLE
35 songs: Cross Road Blues (Crossroads) • Hide Away • The House Is Rockin' • Love Struck Baby • Move It On Over • Piece of My Heart • Statesboro Blues • You Shook Me • more.
00690450...$19.95

CLASSIC ROCK GUITAR BIBLE
33 essential rock songs: Beast of Burden • Cat Scratch Fever • Double Vision • Free Ride • Hard to Handle • Life in the Fast Lane • The Stroke • Won't Get Fooled Again • and more.
00690662...$19.95

COUNTRY GUITAR BIBLE
35 country classics: Ain't Goin' Down • Blue Eyes Crying in the Rain • Boot Scootin' Boogie • Friends in Low Places • I'm So Lonesome I Could Cry • T-R-O-U-B-L-E • and more.
00690465...$19.95

DISCO GUITAR BIBLE
30 stand-out songs from the disco days: Brick House • Disco Inferno • Funkytown • Get Down Tonight • I Love the Night Life • Le Freak • Stayin' Alive • Y.M.C.A. • and more.
00690627...$17.95

EARLY ROCK GUITAR BIBLE
35 fantastic classics: Blue Suede Shoes • Do Wah Diddy Diddy • Hang On Sloopy • I'm a Believer • Louie, Louie • Oh, Pretty Woman • Surfin' U.S.A. • Twist and Shout • and more.
00690680...$17.95

FOLK-ROCK GUITAR BIBLE
35 songs: At Seventeen • Blackbird • Fire and Rain • Happy Together • Leaving on a Jet Plane • Our House • Time in a Bottle • Turn! Turn! Turn! • You've Got a Friend • more.
00690464...$19.95

GRUNGE GUITAR BIBLE
30 songs: All Apologies • Counting Blue Cars • Glycerine • Jesus Christ Pose • Lithium • Man in the Box • Nearly Lost You • Smells like Teen Spirit • This Is a Call • Violet • and more.
00690649...$17.95

HARD ROCK GUITAR BIBLE
35 songs: Ballroom Blitz • Bang a Gong • Barracuda • Living After Midnight • Rock You like a Hurricane • School's Out • Welcome to the Jungle • You Give Love a Bad Name • more.
00690453...$19.95

INSTRUMENTAL GUITAR BIBLE
37 great instrumentals: Always with Me, Always with You • Green Onions • Hide Away • Jessica • Linus and Lucy • Perfidia • Satch Boogie • Tequila • Walk Don't Run • and more.
00690514...$19.95

JAZZ GUITAR BIBLE
31 songs: Body and Soul • In a Sentimental Mood • My Funny Valentine • Nuages • Satin Doll • So What • Star Dust • Take Five • Tangerine • Yardbird Suite • and more.
00690466...$19.95

MODERN ROCK GUITAR BIBLE
26 rock favorites: Aerials (System of a Down) • Alive (P.O.D.) • Cold Hard Bitch (Jet) • Kryptonite (3 Doors Down) • Like a Stone (Audioslave) • Whatever (Godsmack) • and more.
00690724...$19.95

NÜ METAL GUITAR BIBLE
25 edgy metal hits: Aenema • Black • Edgecrusher • Last Resort • People of the Sun • Schism • Southtown • Take a Look Around • Toxicity • Youth of the Nation • and more.
00690569...$19.95

POP/ROCK GUITAR BIBLE
35 pop hits: Change the World • Heartache Tonight • Money for Nothing • Mony, Mony • Pink Houses • Smooth • Summer of '69 • 3 AM • What I Like About You • and more.
00690517...$19.95

R&B GUITAR BIBLE
35 R&B classics: Brick House • Fire • I Got You (I Feel Good) • Love Rollercoaster • Shining Star • Sir Duke • Super Freak • and more.
00690452...$19.95

ROCK GUITAR BIBLE
33 songs: All Day and All of the Night • Born to Be Wild • Day Tripper • Hey Joe • Jailhouse Rock • Money • Paranoid • Sultans of Swing • Walk This Way • You Really Got Me • more!
00690313...$19.95

ROCKABILLY GUITAR BIBLE
31 songs from artists such as Elvis, Buddy Holly and the Brian Setzer Orchestra: Blue Suede Shoes • Hello Mary Lou • Peggy Sue • Rock This Town • Travelin' Man • and more.
00690570...$19.95

SOUL GUITAR BIBLE
33 songs: Groovin' • I've Been Loving You Too Long • Let's Get It On • My Girl • Respect • Theme from Shaft • Soul Man • and more.
00690506...$19.95

SOUTHERN ROCK GUITAR BIBLE
25 southern rock classics: Can't You See • Free Bird • Hold On Loosely • La Grange • Midnight Rider • Sweet Home Alabama • and more.
00690723...$19.95

Prices, contents, and availability subject to change without notice.

FOR MORE INFORMATION, SEE YOUR LOCAL MUSIC DEALER, OR WRITE TO:

HAL•LEONARD®
CORPORATION
7777 W. BLUEMOUND RD. P.O. BOX 13819 MILWAUKEE, WI 53213

Visit Hal Leonard online at **www.halleonard.com**

0606

HAL•LEONARD GUITAR PLAY-ALONG

This series will help you play your favorite songs quickly and easily. Just follow the tab and listen to the CD to hear how the guitar should sound, and then play along using the separate backing tracks. Mac or PC users can also slow down the tempo without changing pitch by using the CD in their computer. The melody and lyrics are included in the book so that you can sing or simply follow along.

INCLUDES TAB

VOL. 1 – ROCK GUITAR 00699570 / $14.95
Day Tripper • Message in a Bottle • Refugee • Shattered • Sunshine of Your Love • Takin' Care of Business • Tush • Walk This Way.

VOL. 2 – ACOUSTIC 00699569 / $14.95
Angie • Behind Blue Eyes • Best of My Love • Blackbird • Dust in the Wind • Layla • Night Moves • Yesterday.

VOL. 3 – HARD ROCK 00699573 / $14.95
Crazy Train • Iron Man • Living After Midnight • Rock You like a Hurricane • Round and Round • Smoke on the Water • Sweet Child O' Mine • You Really Got Me.

VOL. 4 – POP/ROCK 00699571 / $14.95
Breakdown • Crazy Little Thing Called Love • Hit Me with Your Best Shot • I Want You to Want Me • Lights • R.O.C.K. in the U.S.A. • Summer of '69 • What I Like About You.

VOL. 5 – MODERN ROCK 00699574 / $14.95
Aerials • Alive • Bother • Chop Suey! • Control • Last Resort • Take a Look Around (Theme from *M:I-2*) • Wish You Were Here.

VOL. 6 – '90S ROCK 00699572 / $14.95
Are You Gonna Go My Way • Come Out and Play • I'll Stick Around • Know Your Enemy • Man in the Box • Outshined • Smells Like Teen Spirit • Under the Bridge.

VOL. 7 – BLUES GUITAR 00699575 / $14.95
All Your Love (I Miss Loving) • Born Under a Bad Sign • Hide Away • I'm Tore Down • I'm Your Hoochie Coochie Man • Pride and Joy • Sweet Home Chicago • The Thrill Is Gone.

VOL. 8 – ROCK 00699585 / $14.95
All Right Now • Black Magic Woman • Get Back • Hey Joe • Layla • Love Me Two Times • Won't Get Fooled Again • You Really Got Me.

VOL. 9 – PUNK ROCK 00699576 / $14.95
All the Small Things • Fat Lip • Flavor of the Weak • I Feel So • Lifestyles of the Rich and Famous • Say It Ain't So • Self Esteem • (So) Tired of Waiting for You.

VOL. 10 – ACOUSTIC 00699586 / $14.95
Here Comes the Sun • Landslide • The Magic Bus • Norwegian Wood (This Bird Has Flown) • Pink Houses • Space Oddity • Tangled Up in Blue • Tears in Heaven.

VOL. 11 – EARLY ROCK 00699579 / $14.95
Fun, Fun, Fun • Hound Dog • Louie, Louie • No Particular Place to Go • Oh, Pretty Woman • Rock Around the Clock • Under the Boardwalk • Wild Thing.

VOL. 12 – POP/ROCK 00699587 / $14.95
867-5309/Jenny • Every Breath You Take • Money for Nothing • Rebel, Rebel • Run to You • Ticket to Ride • Wonderful Tonight • You Give Love a Bad Name.

VOL. 13 – FOLK ROCK 00699581 / $14.95
Annie's Song • Leaving on a Jet Plane • Suite: Judy Blue Eyes • This Land Is Your Land • Time in a Bottle • Turn! Turn! Turn! • You've Got a Friend • You've Got to Hide Your Love Away.

VOL. 14 – BLUES ROCK 00699582 / $14.95
Blue on Black • Crossfire • Cross Road Blues (Crossroads) • The House Is Rockin' • La Grange • Move It on Over • Roadhouse Blues • Statesboro Blues.

VOL. 15 – R&B 00699583 / $14.95
Ain't Too Proud to Beg • Brick House • Get Ready • I Can't Help Myself • I Got You (I Feel Good) • I Heard It Through the Grapevine • My Girl • Shining Star.

VOL. 16 – JAZZ 00699584 / $14.95
All Blues • Bluesette • Footprints • How Insensitive • Misty • Satin Doll • Stella by Starlight • Tenor Madness.

VOL. 17 – COUNTRY 00699588 / $14.95
Amie • Boot Scootin' Boogie • Chattahoochee • Folsom Prison Blues • Friends in Low Places • Forever and Ever, Amen • T-R-O-U-B-L-E • Workin' Man Blues.

VOL. 18 – ACOUSTIC ROCK 00699577 / $14.95
About a Girl • Breaking the Girl • Drive • Iris • More Than Words • Patience • Silent Lucidity • 3 AM.

VOL. 19 – SOUL 00699578 / $14.95
Get Up (I Feel Like Being) a Sex Machine • Green Onions • In the Midnight Hour • Knock on Wood • Mustang Sally • Respect • (Sittin' On) The Dock of the Bay • Soul Man.

VOL. 20 – ROCKABILLY 00699580 / $14.95
Be-Bop-A-Lula • Blue Suede Shoes • Hello Mary Lou • Little Sister • Mystery Train • Rock This Town • Stray Cat Strut • That'll Be the Day.

VOL. 21 – YULETIDE 00699602 / $14.95
Angels We Have Heard on High • Away in a Manger • Deck the Hall • The First Noel • Go, Tell It on the Mountain • Jingle Bells • Joy to the World • O Little Town of Bethlehem.

VOL. 22 – CHRISTMAS 00699600 / $14.95
The Christmas Song • Frosty the Snow Man • Happy Xmas • Here Comes Santa Claus • Jingle-Bell Rock • Merry Christmas, Darling • Rudolph the Red-Nosed Reindeer • Silver Bells.

VOL. 23 – SURF 00699635 / $14.95
Let's Go Trippin' • Out of Limits • Penetration • Pipeline • Surf City • Surfin' U.S.A. • Walk Don't Run • The Wedge.

VOL. 24 – ERIC CLAPTON 00699649 / $14.95
Badge • Bell Bottom Blues • Change the World • Cocaine • Key to the Highway • Lay Down Sally • White Room • Wonderful Tonight.

VOL. 25 – LENNON & McCARTNEY 00699642 / $14.95
Back in the U.S.S.R. • Drive My Car • Get Back • A Hard Day's Night • I Feel Fine • Paperback Writer • Revolution • Ticket to Ride.

VOL. 26 – ELVIS PRESLEY 00699643 / $14.95
All Shook Up • Blue Suede Shoes • Don't Be Cruel • Heartbreak Hotel • Hound Dog • Jailhouse Rock • Little Sister • Mystery Train.

VOL. 27 – DAVID LEE ROTH 00699645 / $14.95
Ain't Talkin' 'Bout Love • Dance the Night Away • Hot for Teacher • Just Like Paradise • A Lil' Ain't Enough • Runnin' with the Devil • Unchained • Yankee Rose.

VOL. 28 – GREG KOCH 00699646 / $14.95
Chief's Blues • Death of a Bassman • Dylan the Villain • The Grip • Holy Grail • Spank It • Tonus Diabolicus • Zoiks.

VOL. 29 – BOB SEGER 00699647 / $14.95
Against the Wind • Betty Lou's Gettin' Out Tonight • Hollywood Nights • Mainstreet • Night Moves • Old Time Rock & Roll • Rock and Roll Never Forgets • Still the Same.

VOL. 30 – KISS 00699644 / $14.95
Cold Gin • Detroit Rock City • Deuce • Firehouse • Heaven's on Fire • Love Gun • Rock and Roll All Nite • Shock Me.

VOL. 31 – CHRISTMAS HITS 00699652 / $14.95
Blue Christmas • Do You Hear What I Hear • Happy Holiday • I Saw Mommy Kissing Santa Claus • I'll Be Home for Christmas • Let It Snow! Let It Snow! Let It Snow! • Little Saint Nick • Snowfall.

VOL. 32 – THE OFFSPRING 00699653 / $14.95
Bad Habit • Come Out and Play • Gone Away • Gotta Get Away • Hit That • The Kids Aren't Alright • Pretty Fly (For a White Guy) • Self Esteem.

VOL. 33 – ACOUSTIC CLASSICS 00699656 / $14.95
Across the Universe • Babe, I'm Gonna Leave You • Crazy on You • Heart of Gold • Hotel California • I'd Love to Change the World • Thick As a Brick • Wanted Dead or Alive.

VOL. 34 – CLASSIC ROCK 00699658 / $14.95
Aqualung • Born to Be Wild • The Boys Are Back in Town • Brown Eyed Girl • Reeling in the Years • Rock'n Me • Rocky Mountain Way • Sweet Emotion.

VOL. 35 – HAIR METAL 00699660 / $14.95
Decadence Dance • Don't Treat Me Bad • Down Boys • Seventeen • Shake Me • Up All Night • Wait • Talk Dirty to Me.

VOL. 36 – SOUTHERN ROCK 00699661 / $14.95
Can't You See • Flirtin' with Disaster • Hold on Loosely • Jessica • Mississippi Queen • Ramblin' Man • Sweet Home Alabama • What's Your Name.

VOL. 37 – ACOUSTIC METAL 00699662 / $14.95
Every Rose Has Its Thorn • Fly to the Angels • Hole Hearted • Love Is on the Way • Love of a Lifetime • Signs • To Be with You • When the Children Cry.

VOL. 38 – BLUES 00699663 / $14.95
Boom Boom • Cold Shot • Crosscut Saw • Everyday I Have the Blues • Frosty • Further On up the Road • Killing Floor • Texas Flood.

VOL. 39 – '80S METAL 00699664 / $14.95
Bark at the Moon • Big City Nights • Breaking the Chains • Cult of Personality • Lay It Down • Living on a Prayer • Panama • Smokin' in the Boys Room.

VOL. 40 – INCUBUS 00699668 / $14.95
Are You In? • Drive • Megalomaniac • Nice to Know You • Pardon Me • Stellar • Talk Shows on Mute • Wish You Were Here.

VOL. 41 – ERIC CLAPTON 00699669 / $14.95
After Midnight • Can't Find My Way Home • Forever Man • I Shot the Sheriff • I'm Tore Down • Pretending • Running on Faith • Tears in Heaven.

VOL. 42 – CHART HITS 00699670 / $14.95
Are You Gonna Be My Girl • Heaven • Here Without You • I Believe in a Thing Called Love • Just Like You • Last Train Home • This Love • Until the Day I Die.

VOL. 43 – LYNYRD SKYNYRD 00699681 / $14.95
Don't Ask Me No Questions • Free Bird • Gimme Three Steps • I Know a Little • Saturday Night Special • Sweet Home Alabama • That Smell • You Got That Right.

VOL. 44 – JAZZ 00699689 / $14.95
I Remember You • I'll Remember April • Impressions • In a Mellow Tone • Moonlight in Vermont • On a Slow Boat to China • Things Ain't What They Used to Be • Yesterdays.

VOL. 46 – MAINSTREAM ROCK 00699722 / $14.95
Just a Girl • Keep Away • Kryptonite • Lightning Crashes • 1979 • One Step Closer • Scar Tissue • Torn.

VOL. 47 – HENDRIX SMASH HITS 00699723/ $16.95
All Along the Watchtower • Can You See Me? • Crosstown Traffic • Fire • Foxey Lady • Hey Joe • Manic Depression • Purple Haze • Red House • Remember • Stone Free • The Wind Cries Mary.

VOL. 48 – AEROSMITH CLASSICS 00699724 / $14.95
Back in the Saddle • Draw the Line • Dream On • Last Child • Mama Kin • Same Old Song & Dance • Sweet Emotion • Walk This Way.

VOL. 50 – NÜ METAL 00699726 / $14.95
Duality • Here to Stay • In the End • Judith • Nookie • So Cold • Toxicity • Whatever.

VOL. 51 – ALTERNATIVE '90S 00699727 / $14.95
Alive • Cherub Rock • Come As You Are • Give It Away • Jane Says • No Excuses • No Rain • Santeria.

VOL. 56 – FOO FIGHTERS 00699749 / $14.95
All My Life • Best of You • DOA • I'll Stick Around • Learn to Fly • Monkey Wrench • My Hero • This Is a Call.

VOL. 57 – SYSTEM OF A DOWN 00699751 / $14.95
Aerials • B.Y.O.B. • Chop Suey! • Innervision • Question! • Spiders • Sugar • Toxicity.

Prices, contents, and availability subject to change without notice.

00694757 Yngwie Malmsteen – Trilogy	$19.95	
00694754 Marilyn Manson – Lest We Forget	$19.95	
00694956 Bob Marley – Legend	$19.95	
00690075 Bob Marley – Natural Mystic	$19.95	
00690548 Very Best of Bob Marley & The Wailers – One Love	$19.95	
00694945 Bob Marley – Songs of Freedom	$24.95	
00690748 Maroon5 – 1.22.03 Acoustic	$19.95	
00690657 Maroon5 – Songs About Jane	$19.95	
00690442 Matchbox 20 – Mad Season	$19.95	
00690616 Matchbox 20 – More Than You Think You Are	$19.95	
00690239 Matchbox 20 – Yourself or Someone Like You	$19.95	
00690283 Best of Sarah McLachlan	$19.95	
00690382 Sarah McLachlan – Mirrorball	$19.95	
00690354 Sarah McLachlan – Surfacing	$19.95	
00120080 Don McLean Songbook	$19.95	
00694952 Megadeth – Countdown to Extinction	$19.95	
00690244 Megadeth – Cryptic Writings	$19.95	
00694951 Megadeth – Rust in Peace	$22.95	
00694953 Megadeth – Selections from Peace Sells...But Who's Buying? & So Far, So Good...So What!	$22.95	
00690768 Megadeth – The System Has Failed	$19.95	
00690495 Megadeth – The World Needs a Hero	$19.95	
00690011 Megadeth – Youthanasia	$19.95	
00690505 John Mellencamp Guitar Collection	$19.95	
00690562 Pat Metheny – Bright Size Life	$19.95	
00690646 Pat Metheny – One Quiet Night	$19.95	
00690559 Pat Metheny – Question & Answer	$19.95	
00690565 Pat Metheny – Rejoicing	$19.95	
00690558 Pat Metheny Trio – 99>00	$19.95	
00690561 Pat Metheny Trio – Live	$22.95	
00690040 Steve Miller Band Greatest Hits	$19.95	
00690769 Modest Mouse – Good News for People Who Love Bad News	$19.95	
00694802 Gary Moore – Still Got the Blues	$19.95	
00690103 Alanis Morissette – Jagged Little Pill	$19.95	
00690786 Mudvayne – The End of All Things to Come	$22.95	
00690787 Mudvayne – L.D. 50	$22.95	
00690794 Mudvayne – Lost and Found	$19.95	
00690500 MxPx – The Ever Passing Moment	$19.95	
00690500 Ricky Nelson Guitar Collection	$17.95	
00690722 New Found Glory – Catalyst	$19.95	
00690345 Best of Newsboys	$17.95	
00690611 Nirvana	$22.95	
00694895 Nirvana – Bleach	$19.95	
00690189 Nirvana – From the Muddy Banks of the Wishkah	$19.95	
00694913 Nirvana – In Utero	$19.95	
00694901 Nirvana – Incesticide	$19.95	
00694883 Nirvana – Nevermind	$19.95	
00690026 Nirvana – Unplugged in York	$19.95	
00690739 No Doubt – Rock Steady	$22.95	
00120112 No Doubt – Tragic Kingdom	$22.95	
00690273 Oasis – Be Here Now	$19.95	
00690159 Oasis – Definitely Maybe	$19.95	
00690121 Oasis – (What's the Story) Morning Glory	$19.95	
00690226 Oasis – The Other Side of Oasis	$19.95	
00690358 The Offspring – Americana	$19.95	
00690485 The Offspring – Conspiracy of One	$19.95	
00690807 The Offspring – Greatest Hits	$19.95	
00690204 The Offspring – Ixnay on the Hombre	$17.95	
00690203 The Offspring – Smash	$18.95	
00690663 The Offspring – Splinter	$19.95	
00694847 Best of Ozzy Osbourne	$22.95	
00694830 Ozzy Osbourne – No More Tears	$19.95	
00690399 Ozzy Osbourne – The Ozzman Cometh	$19.95	
00690129 Ozzy Osbourne – Ozzmosis	$22.95	
00690594 Best of Les Paul	$19.95	
00690546 P.O.D. – Satellite	$19.95	
00694855 Pearl Jam – Ten	$19.95	
00690439 A Perfect Circle – Mer De Noms	$19.95	
00690661 A Perfect Circle – Thirteenth Step	$19.95	
00690499 Tom Petty – Definitive Guitar Collection	$19.95	
00690176 Phish – Billy Breathes	$22.95	
00690424 Phish – Farmhouse	$19.95	
00690240 Phish – Hoist	$19.95	
00690331 Phish – Story of the Ghost	$19.95	
00690642 Pillar – Fireproof	$19.95	
00690731 Pillar – Where Do We Go from Here	$19.95	
00690428 Pink Floyd – Dark Side of the Moon	$19.95	
00693864 Best of The Police	$19.95	
00690299 Best of Elvis: The King of Rock 'n' Roll	$19.95	
00692535 Elvis Presley	$18.95	
00690003 Classic Queen	$24.95	
00694975 Queen – Greatest Hits	$24.95	
00690670 Very Best of Queensryche	$19.95	
00694910 Rage Against the Machine	$19.95	
00690145 Rage Against the Machine – Evil Empire	$19.95	
00690179 Rancid – And Out Come the Wolves	$22.95	
00690426 Best of Ratt	$19.95	
00690055 Red Hot Chili Peppers – Bloodsugarsexmagik	$19.95	
00690584 Red Hot Chili Peppers – By the Way	$19.95	
00690379 Red Hot Chili Peppers – Californication	$19.95	
00690673 Red Hot Chili Peppers – Greatest Hits	$19.95	
00690255 Red Hot Chili Peppers – Mother's Milk	$19.95	
00690090 Red Hot Chili Peppers – One Hot Minute	$22.95	
00690511 Django Reinhardt – The Definitive Collection	$19.95	
00690779 Relient K – MMHMM	$19.95	
00690643 Relient K – Two Lefts Don't Make a Right ... But Three Do	$19.95	
00694899 R.E.M. – Automatic for the People	$19.95	
00690260 Jimmie Rodgers Guitar Collection	$19.95	
00690014 Rolling Stones – Exile on Main Street	$24.95	
00690631 Rolling Stones – Guitar Anthology	$24.95	
00690186 Rolling Stones – Rock & Roll Circus	$19.95	
00690685 David Lee Roth – Eat 'Em and Smile	$19.95	
00690694 David Lee Roth – Guitar Anthology	$24.95	
00690749 Saliva – Survival of the Sickest	$19.95	
00690031 Santana's Greatest Hits	$19.95	
00690796 Very Best of Michael Schenker	$19.95	
00690566 Best of Scorpions	$19.95	
00690604 Bob Seger – Guitar Anthology	$19.95	
00690659 Bob Seger and the Silver Bullet Band – Greatest Hits, Volume 2	$17.95	
00120105 Kenny Wayne Shepherd – Ledbetter Heights	$19.95	
00690750 Kenny Wayne Shepherd – The Place You're In	$19.95	
00120123 Kenny Wayne Shepherd – Trouble Is	$19.95	
00690196 Silverchair – Freak Show	$19.95	
00690130 Silverchair – Frogstomp	$19.95	
00690357 Silverchair – Neon Ballroom	$19.95	
00690419 Slipknot	$19.95	
00690530 Slipknot – Iowa	$19.95	
00690733 Slipknot – Volume 3 (The Subliminal Verses)	$19.95	
00690691 Smashing Pumpkins Anthology	$19.95	
00690330 Social Distortion – Live at the Roxy	$19.95	
00120004 Best of Steely Dan	$24.95	
00694921 Best of Steppenwolf	$22.95	
00690655 Best of Mike Stern	$19.95	
00694801 Best of Rod Stewart	$22.95	
00694957 Rod Stewart – Unplugged...And Seated	$22.95	
00690021 Sting – Fields of Gold	$19.95	
00694955 Sting for Guitar Tab	$19.95	
00690597 Stone Sour	$19.95	
00690689 Story of the Year – Page Avenue	$19.95	
00690520 Styx Guitar Collection	$19.95	
00120081 Sublime	$19.95	
00690519 SUM 41 – All Killer No Filler	$19.95	
00690771 SUM 41 – Chuck	$19.95	
00690612 SUM 41 – Does This Look Infected?	$19.95	
00690767 Switchfoot – The Beautiful Letdown	$19.95	
00690815 Switchfoot – Nothing Is Sound	$19.95	
00690425 System of a Down	$19.95	
00690799 System of a Down – Mezmerize	$19.95	
00690606 System of a Down – Steal This Album	$19.95	
00690531 System of a Down – Toxicity	$19.95	
00694824 Best of James Taylor	$16.95	
00694887 Best of Thin Lizzy	$19.95	
00690238 Third Eye Blind	$19.95	
00690671 Three Days Grace	$19.95	
00690738 3 Doors Down – Away from the Sun	$22.95	
00690737 3 Doors Down – The Better Life	$22.95	
00690776 3 Doors Down – Seventeen Days	$19.95	
00690267 311	$19.95	
00690580 311 – From Chaos	$19.95	
00690269 311 – Grass Roots	$19.95	
00690268 311 – Music	$19.95	
00690665 Thursday – War All the Time	$19.95	
00690030 Toad the Wet Sprocket	$19.95	
00690654 Best of Train	$19.95	
00690233 Merle Travis Collection	$19.95	
00690683 Robin Trower – Bridge of Sighs	$19.95	
00690740 Shania Twain – Guitar Collection	$19.95	
00699191 U2 – Best of: 1980-1990	$19.95	
00690732 U2 – Best of: 1990-2000	$19.95	
00690775 U2 – How to Dismantle an Atomic Bomb	$22.95	
00694411 U2 – The Joshua Tree	$19.95	
00690039 Steve Vai – Alien Love Secrets	$24.95	
00690172 Steve Vai – Fire Garden	$24.95	
00690343 Steve Vai – Flex-able Leftovers	$19.95	
00660137 Steve Vai – Passion & Warfare	$24.95	
00690605 Steve Vai – Selections from the Elusive Light and Sound, Volume 1	$24.95	
00694904 Steve Vai – Sex and Religion	$24.95	
00690392 Steve Vai – The Ultra Zone	$22.95	
00690023 Jimmie Vaughan – Strange Pleasures	$19.95	
00690455 Stevie Ray Vaughan – Blues at Sunrise	$19.95	
00690024 Stevie Ray Vaughan – Couldn't Stand the Weather	$19.95	
00690370 Stevie Ray Vaughan and Double Trouble – The Real Deal: Greatest Hits Volume 2	$22.95	
00690116 Stevie Ray Vaughan – Guitar Collection	$24.95	
00660136 Stevie Ray Vaughan – In Step	$19.95	
00694879 Stevie Ray Vaughan – In the Beginning	$19.95	
00660058 Stevie Ray Vaughan – Lightnin' Blues '83-'87	$24.95	
00690036 Stevie Ray Vaughan – Live Alive	$24.95	
00690417 Stevie Ray Vaughan – Live at Carnegie Hall	$19.95	
00690550 Stevie Ray Vaughan and Double Trouble – Live at Montreux 1982 & 1985	$24.95	
00694835 Stevie Ray Vaughan – The Sky Is Crying	$22.95	
00690025 Stevie Ray Vaughan – Soul to Soul	$19.95	
00690015 Stevie Ray Vaughan – Texas Flood	$19.95	
00694776 Vaughan Brothers – Family Style	$19.95	
00690772 Velvet Revolver – Contraband	$19.95	
00690132 The T-Bone Walker Collection	$19.95	
00694789 Muddy Waters – Deep Blues	$24.95	
00690071 Weezer (The Blue Album)	$19.95	
00690516 Weezer (The Green Album)	$19.95	
00690800 Weezer – Make Believe	$19.95	
00690286 Weezer – Pinkerton	$19.95	
00690447 Best of The Who	$24.95	
00694970 The Who – Definitive Guitar Collection: A-E	$24.95	
00694971 The Who – Definitive Guitar Collection: F-Li	$24.95	
00694972 The Who – Definitive Guitar Collection: Lo-R	$24.95	
00694973 The Who – Definitive Guitar Collection: S-Y	$24.95	
00690640 David Wilcox – Anthology 2000-2003	$19.95	
00690325 David Wilcox – Collection	$17.95	
00690672 Best of Dar Williams	$19.95	
00690320 Dar Williams Songbook	$17.95	
00690319 Stevie Wonder – Some of the Best	$17.95	
00690596 Best of the Yardbirds	$19.95	
00690710 Yellowcard – Ocean Avenue	$19.95	
00690507 Frank Zappa – Apostrophe	$19.95	
00690443 Frank Zappa – Hot Rats	$19.95	
00690589 ZZ Top – Guitar Anthology	$22.95